Design for Church Growth

DESIGN FOR CHURCH GROWTH

**Charles L. Chaney
Ron S. Lewis**

BROADMAN PRESS
Nashville, Tennessee

4262-18
ISBN: 0-8054-6218-x

Dewey Decimal Classification: 254.5
Subject heading: CHURCH GROWTH
Library of Congress Catalog Card Number: 77-87364
Printed in the United States of America

Preface

This small book about the growth of the church of Jesus Christ demands a word of explanation to set it in perspective. Churches are organisms, living bodies with dynamic parts that interact. Growth only takes place where life exists. Church growth, then, is a complex and multidimensional affair, a subject that cannot be adequately covered in a few pages. This book is concerned with one dimension of the larger subject, and you should know that before you begin. It is *not* about church growth in its multidimensional totality. So please avoid judging it from that viewpoint.

What we say in these pages is intended for local churches and designed to be exceedingly pragmatic. The principles we discuss will apply to larger expressions of the church, such as local associations or synods, national conferences or conventions, or international ecclesiastical bodies. But these are not our target group. Local congregations man the front lines of evangelism and the staging areas of building up the body of Christ. The effectiveness in equipping the saints and in communicating Christ to the pagan pools of humanity determines how the battle against the kingdom of darkness proceeds in any generation. This book is intended to provide very practical assistance to those local congregations whose life is marked by an evangelical passion to bring all men to obedience to Jesus Christ.

Biblical material for growing churches and the historical experience of churches demands a comprehensive definition of church growth. We define church growth in its totality as the process in which a church grows into Christ's fullness, that movement toward the "measure of the stature of the fullness of Christ" in all of the cultures of man. Christian parents are concerned that their childen grow physically, mentally, socially, and spiritually. They express anxiety when any one of these four is lacking. So, churches grow in various ways and it is important that balance be maintained.

66328

Alan R. Tippett, a decade ago, in his classic study, *Solomon Islands Christianity* [1] and Orlando E. Costas in his report to the Lausanne Congress on World Evangelization [2] and, more recently, in *The Church and Its Mission*,[3] have put Christians in their debt by their work at this point. At least four dimensions of church growth have been identified and described.

1. *Numerical growth* is the perpetual ingathering of new disciples of Jesus Christ into the fellowship of local congregations or the gathering of new believers into new churches. Numerical growth is directly and uniquely related to conversion from the world—whether the world of religions, humanism, materialism, agnosticism, or nominal Christianity. In numerical growth individuals are introduced to Jesus Christ, choose to believe in him and to deliberately declare allegiance to him and his people. They are baptized and incorporated into the church's life.

2. *Organic growth* has to do with the development of the church or a community. It concerns the internal structure of relationships within the body itself. The choice of the seven (Acts 6:1–7) and the sending out of Barnabas and Saul by the church of Antioch (Acts 13:1–13) are both an expression of organic growth. The natural development of organizations in a church to perform its ministry and fulfill its mission is evidence of organic growth. Organic growth includes the development of leadership, the rise and restructure of organizations, and the emergence of the congregation to an indigenous and independent existence in the community.

3. *Maturational growth* could be technically referred to as *telesphoric growth*. It refers to the movement toward perfection or maturity (*teleos*) about which the New Testament speaks often (1 Cor. 2:6; 3:1; 13:11; Eph. 4:14, Phil. 3:15; Heb. 5:14; 6:1). Maturational growth is both conceptual and behavioral. A church grows in its understanding of the Word of God and the application of the Word of God to the situations of life. Reflection and demonstration are the two arenas in which spiritual maturity is expressed. Having the mind of Christ and manifesting his holy life are the goals of this internal, qualitative dimension of church growth.

4. *Incarnational growth* is that expansion of the church which is seen by its effect on its environment. It too has a dual expression. The church is growing when it intensifies its participation in the afflictions of humanity [4] and when it is able to exhibit the character of Jesus in the culture of that people where it is planted. These two aspects of incarnational growth must always be in creative tension. A church can be taken captive to its culture and never speak prophetically to is generation or become involved

in lifting up the downtrodden and dispossessed. A church may be immersed in the fight for justice but always remain alive and paternalistic. One dimension of church growth is related to the progress of the church in seeing both the compassion and character of Jesus manifest in the various human cultures.

This book is about *numerical* growth. In it, we define church growth as *the numerical increase of local congregations through making disciples of those not yet obedient to Jesus Christ as Lord and multiplying new congregations among all peoples and in all places where these are needed.*

We make no apology for focusing on this aspect of the growth of the church. For this is the one dimension of church growth that is absolutely essential to all the rest. There can be no perfecting of the saints without saints. No organic growth can take place without the building blocks with which to develop structure. Real substance, actual quantity, is prerequisite to the incarnation of a church in the culture where it is planted and the molding of society after the image of Christ.

Numerical growth is fundamental and integral to God's intention to take from "among the nations a people" for himself (Acts 15:14). Numerical growth is, therefore, the essential and irreplaceable element in the mission of the church. A church is not fulfilling its mission, is not obedient to that for which it is sent, if it is not making disciples to Jesus Christ and planting churches within each and every ethnic segment of society. We can know how faithful we are being to God in this regard. How are we doing in persuading men to believe in Jesus and become faithful members of his new people?

Finally, numerical growth is the crying need of American Christianity at this hour. At least eighty million people in America give no adherence at all to Jesus Christ. There are only six nations of the world with a population larger than eighty million. Fifty million others are only nominal adherents. They are Christians, not because of any personal relationship to Jesus Christ, but because they are not Buddhists or Muslims or animists. To have their name on some church roll has not changed their life a whit. These 130 million need our attention. What must we do to make some impact on this group? is the question we will ask over and over.

In reality, since the late 50s, most American churches have been caught up in the maintenance syndrome. This mentality asks, "How can we hold what we have and improve its quality?" For the last ten years many churches have been in decline. Hundreds have gone out of existence. It is impossible to have quality without quantity, and the millions of Americans who do not know Jesus Christ as personal Savior and Lord wait for us to present them with this truth.

CHARLES CHANEY

RON S. LEWIS

July, 1977

Contents

Abbreviations and Translations

1
Every Church Can Grow

Church-in-a-huge-city was organized in 1967. It had twenty-six members and great hopes. It met in the rented space of a semibasement storefront. Thousands of people were in walking distance of its doors. In 1973, six years later, it had twenty-three members. In 1977, the church disbanded. It never grew.

Church-in-a-growing suburb was organized in 1959. It was one of the first churches constituted in a new suburban city. It secured an excellent site and built a beautiful building. Growth was slow but steady, from fifty-five members to 230, during the first decade. During the last six years (1975) membership has declined to 204. Its growth has been arrested. It is on a growth plateau with a slight slope down. The city is and has been one of the fastest growing cities in the state. The city population has grown from 9,046 in 1960 to 28,516 in 1975.

Church-in-a-major-city was organized in 1948. Eighty-five members, transferred from another church in the city, became the nucleus of the new congregation. During the first decade membership grew to 510. By 1968, during the second decade, membership declined to 460. During the past seven years, total membership has gone to 710, but Sunday School enrollment and Sunday attendance have declined to 349 and 165 respectively. This church has, in fact, declined during the larger portion of its third decade.

The Perplexing Problem

These three churches all illustrate a perplexing problem: *little or no growth in many churches!*

Why do churches stand still? Why, though planted in a huge field of people needing Jesus Christ, do churches either never grow, cease to grow, or begin to decline?

The experience of other churches (some churches grow consistently and often dramatically) and the teaching of the New Testament contradict

15

this prevalent modern pattern. The witness of the New Testament as a whole is clear:

1. Every church should grow!
2. Every church can grow!

These two statements say what this chapter—indeed, what this book—is all about. Growth is a sign of *life* and *health*. Nongrowth is evidence of *death* and *sickness*. The lack of growth is a malady that need not afflict the body of Christ or any particular local expression of Christ's body. Given an immediate or extended community with unchurched people and given an opportunity openly or clandestinely to share the good news with that population, Christians should expect their church to grow. If a church is not growing, it is imperative that its members take a hard look at the reasons for nongrowth. Efforts must be made to diagnose the health of their church. Churches are not intended to be stunted and stagnant in the world. The sickness need not persist!

Grounds for Growth

On what basis do we make such an assertion? Why insist on something that so many find threatening?

We could answer with an analogy from biology. At the entrance of the exhibit area of Chicago's mammoth Shedd Aquarium, there is a plaque which says:

What is life? What is a living thing?

A living thing will exhibit all four of these properties: *growth,* an increase in size and weight from within; *reproduction,* the producing of new individuals or the adding of new units to the colony; *metabolism,* all the chemical and physical processes by which living things use and release energy; and *irritability,* the response to a stimulus using energy from within.

Nonliving things may exhibit some, but never all, of these properties.

We contend that churches are *living things.* They are social organizations, but they are also organisms. The various members have a common life, the Holy Spirit, and a common head, Jesus Christ. The church is his body. Each local church is a visible expression of the whole.

As an organism, we believe churches should exhibit the properties of living things. They should be growing in "size and weight." They should be producing "baby" churches. They should be capable of storing up and releasing both physical and spiritual energy for the functions of life. They should be responsive to stimulation, able to be inspired and motivated.

A remarkable similarity exists between these biological properties and the various kinds of church growth that we will identify. However, biological analogy is not the primary foundation for the assertion that churches can and should grow. Biblical principles provide the grounds for growing churches.

1. *Growth is the work and will of God.*

"What then is Apollos? What is Paul? Servants through whom you believed, as the Lord assigned to each. I planted, Apollos watered, but God gave the growth. So neither he who plants nor he who waters is anything, but only God who gives the growth" (1 Cor. 3:5–7, RSV).

The Lord, himself, adds to the church (Acts 2:47).

2. *Growth is an innate quality of the church of Jesus Christ.*

The church is "built upon the foundation of the apostles and prophets, Christ Jesus himself being the cornerstone, in whom the whole building, being fitted together is growing into a holy temple in the Lord; in whom you also are being built together into a dwelling of God in the Spirit" (Eph. 2:20–22, NASB).

3. *Growth is of the nature of the gospel.*

Wherever in the world the good news about Jesus is preached in the power of the Holy Spirit, that gospel is "bearing fruit and growing" (Col. 1:6, RSV).

4. *Growth is characteristic of the churches of the New Testament.*

Churches in the first century grew in all kinds of circumstances: in times of great revival and renewal (Acts 2:41); in periods of tension and persecution (4:4); in periods of inner church problems (5:14; 6:1,7); in times of civil and religious peace (9:31); as a result of spontaneous witnessing (11:19–21); as a consequence of organized teaching (11:22–26; 12:24); when the church is built up and strong (16:5); and as a result of planned efforts (19:10,20).

The Growth Debate

There is a great debate today about the nature of church growth. The battle lines are usually drawn between what is called

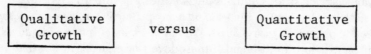

"The key question is not how churches can grow numerically," says one spokesman, "but how they can grow in grace." [1] Indeed, the Bible underscores the need for growth to Christian maturity (Eph. 4:15; Col.

1:10; 1 Pet. 2:2; 2 Pet. 3:18). But this debate is often only a smoke screen to rationalize little or no numerical growth.

A church grows when its members grow in grace. The growth is largely unmeasurable. A church grows when people repent, believe in Jesus Christ, and are baptized and added to the church. This kind of growth is measurable. But the two are not mutually exclusive.

Not either/or but both/and is what is demanded. Qualitative growth and quantitative growth are inseparably related.

1. *Qualitative growth produces quantitative growth,* else something is wrong with its quality. Quality that does not produce quantity is counterfeit.

2. *Quantitative growth makes qualitative growth possible.* There has to be some quantity before there can be quality. Qualitative growth can only exist after the fact of quantitative growth.

3. *Quantitative growth that does not end in qualitative growth will disappear.* Quantitative growth cannot be sustained without taking on the qualitative aspect.

Therefore, the two are not mutual exclusives but mutual dependents. Quantitative growth cannot take place without the dimension of quality. Qualitative growth demands a certain quantity in which to develop quality.

Four Kinds of Church Growth

In reality there are four—not two—kinds of numerical growth.[2] Those who have had a passion to see the church of Jesus Christ increase numerically have often thought only in terms of the expansion of local congregations. This view fails to see the whole body. It also expresses a distorted understanding of "growth" in living things. Growth includes reproduction as well as increasing weight and size.

Whenever a church grows, witnessing and evangelism play a major part. All evangelism is not the same. Different types can be identified in terms of the cultural distances to be crossed before the message has been received. These distinctions are useful in looking at the immediate evangelistic task of churches in America. Failure to recognize these distinctions has kept us from seeing many people in our communities who need to believe on Jesus Christ. We can be guilty of "people blindness." [3] Further, failure to distinguish these levels of evangelism has tied us to ineffective evangelistic strategies for many people. We have been largely unaware of *cultural distance* and have attempted to reach all people with the same methods used with those who are our cultural and social peers.

We will conclude this chapter with a brief introduction to these four kinds of growth and the different types of evangelism that may be involved in effective growth.

1. *Internal growth.*[4]—Internal growth takes place when the church is edified. It is growth in grace and growth toward Christlike maturity. This is that largely immeasurable growth that relates to the quality of a disciples' walk with Christ.

Witness and evangelism may, however, play a part in internal growth. Members of the church may discover they have no lively faith in Christ and meet him in a personal life-changing way. The minor child of devoted church members will be won to faith in Christ. This kind of witnessing may be called *E-0 evangelism,* for no barrier, cultural or otherwise, is crossed in this type of evangelism.[5] Internal growth takes place with the warm fellowship of the local congregation.

2. *Expansion growth.*—Expansion growth takes place when the local congregation expands within its own community. Expansion growth is the numerical increase of a local church.

This growth may come about because of the transfer of those already won to Christ from other areas and/or churches, or it may come from non-Christians converted to faith in Christ, baptized and added to the church. When conversion from the world produces expansion growth, witness and evangelism are major factors. The kind of evangelism most often involved is called *E-1 evangelism* because such growth usually takes place among people of similar culture, language, and social strata. The only barrier crossed is that between Christian and non-Christian.

E-2 evangelism and *E-3 evangelism* may also contribute in expansion growth. If an individual or family is won to Christ from another racial, language, or significantly different socioeconomic group, then two barriers have been crossed—thus, *E-2.* For example, when a traditional white evangelical church persuades an American black family to believe in Christ and become members of their fellowship, they are engaging in

E-2 evangelism. But there are some cultures that are radically different from a witnessing church. If the white evangelical church evangelized a Navajo-speaking family, that is another story. Not only is there a difference in race and culture, the language of the Navajo family is not related in any way to American English. In this case, *E-3 evangelism* is engaged. When these newly won to Christ begin to witness among their own family and cultural community, this witness is always *E-1.* Expansion growth can be accelerated by penetrating multiple homogenous groups or subgroups. In the main, however, expansion growth employs *E-1 evangelism.*

3. *Extension growth.*—Extension growth takes place when the local congregation extends itself to another community and plants a daughter congregation. Extension growth is the gathering of new congregations in adjacent or distant communities.

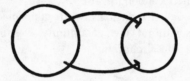

This growth may come about because men and women won to Christ elsewhere are enlisted in the new fellowship or because people are won to Christ and baptized, from that community. Witness and evangelism are central to extension growth. *E-1 evangelism* is most common in extension growth, for extension growth usually happens among people of the same general racial, cultural and socioeconomic strata. The only barrier crossed is that between Christian and non-Christian. But, as in expansion growth, *E-2* and *E-3 evangelism* may also become involved. Extension growth largely explains the explosion by Southern Baptists outside the old Southern states during the last three decades.

4. *Bridging growth.*—Bridging growth takes place when a local congregation plants a daughter congregation within a racial, language or socioeconomic community significantly different from its own. Bridging growth is the gathering of new congregations among people at a significant cultural distance from the mother church. The culturally different community may be immediately adjacent or at some geographical distance from the established church.

Again, some bridging growth may be by transfer of those already Christ's disciples. But, bridging growth most often is closely tied to direct evangelism and significant witness and ministry. The evangelism used may be *E-2* or *E-3.*

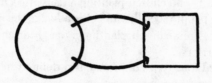

A cultural community may be located in the immediate vicinity of a church, and a daughter congregation may be planted within the mother church's own meeting facilities. However, in most cases it will be in a different geographical community. That which determines whether the evangelism used is E-2 or E-3 has nothing to do with geographical distance. That question is related totally to *cultural distance.* If the racial, cultural or socioeconomic barrier between the witnessing church and the community being evangelized is significant, but still has some points of kinship, the evangelism is *E-2.* If there are no points of kinship, the evangelism is *E-3.*[6]

Evangelism across significant cultural barriers is usually the most difficult type of evangelism. Very often, the help of a person trained to do cross-cultural communication and witnessing is needed. We often call this kind of person a missionary. But many laymen and laywomen are gifted at cross-cultural evangelism and many others can be trained for this ministry.

The purpose of this book is to address itself to *expansion, extension* and *bridging* growth. The program it suggests will relate most specifically to the numerical growth of local congregations (expansion growth), but it will offer challenge and suggest a way that churches may grow through extension and bridging. Every church—we will insist, again and again—should grow. Every church, indeed, CAN grow.

Review

If these statements are true, we are back to our original question: Why do some churches never grow, cease to grow, or begin to decline?

This chapter has introduced many concepts that may be new to you. It is extremely important that you understand the kinds of growth and the types of evangelism defined here and be able to clearly distinguish between them. These terms will occur often in the pages that follow. Let's review them. We said there are four kinds of church growth.

Internal growth is growth in grace and takes place when the church is edified.

Expansion growth is the numerical increase of a local congregation.

Extension growth is one church planting a daughter church in another community, among people socially and culturally like the mother church.

Bridging growth is one church planting a daughter church across significant cultural barriers.

We also identified four types of evangelism defined from the perspective of barriers crossed in communicating Christ.

E-0 evangelism is the type engaged in when the minor children of church members are led to faith in Christ, baptism and church membership, and when those already church members come to personal faith in Christ. These people are already, through their family and church relationship, a "part" of the church. No significant barrier has to be crossed for their conversion. *E-0 evangelism* is a part of the nurturing ministry of the church and should always be part of internal growth.

E-1 evangelism is the type engaged in when people are won to Christ from the world and are essentially in the same cultural and social group as the witnessing church. No cultural barrier has to be crossed, only the barrier between Christian and non-Christian. This is sometimes called the stained-glass barrier. This is winning people to Christ who are basically "like us." *E-1 evangelism* is that most often employed in expansion growth and extension growth.

E-2 evangelism is the type engaged in when people are persuaded to believe in Christ and are added to his church from a significantly, but not totally, different racial, cultural, or socioeconomic community than that of the witnessing church. Two barriers are crossed: the stained-glass barrier and a barrier of racial, cultural, or socioeconomic distance. *E-2 evangelism* is most often employed in bridging growth but may be a part of expansion or extension growth as well.

E-3 evangelism is the type engaged in when people are won to Christ and faithful church membership from a totally different racial, cultural, and language community than the witnessing church. For this person to come to Christ far greater cultural distances have to be overcome. The barrier between Christian and non-Christian must be crossed, but the vast cultural barrier stands before it. Not only is the evangelist "different" from the non-Christian, there is no kinship in culture, language, or race. This utter distinction necessitates *E-3 evangelism*.

2
Limitations to Church Growth

What hinders church growth?

There is no absolute answer to this question. To properly answer this question is to ask other questions: "Which church, in which community, based on what research?"

However, there are some very obvious human barriers to church growth. These characteristics are generally widespread today. Their influence is seen in the growth profiles of far too many churches.

Church growth and nongrowth have at least one characteristic in common. It requires a combination of factors to develop a growing church. The same is true for "nongrowing" churches. Rarely, if ever, can any one factor be the only cause for growth. So it is with nongrowth.

There are limiting factors to church growth. They hinder, stifle, hold back, resist the numerical and inner growth of the church. Some of these hindrances are very subtle. They can only be discovered by careful analysis. Others are very obvious and can be dealt with quickly and adequately. The more subtle ones must be watched for on a regular basis. But, regular record-keeping systems rarely point these out. Periodic analysis must be used to discover them. The factors which are most obvious are those which surface through the use of week-by-week records. When there are not as many present on a given Sunday as there were the same Sunday one year ago, anyone can notice this. But, when these questions are asked: "Why?" "What has caused this?" "Who were those absent?" "What age were they?" and "What was the attendance two years ago?" new factors begin to emerge. A combination of these factors becomes the basis for an explanation for the nongrowth situation.

Keep in mind there are no simple explanations for all nongrowth in the church. Hindrances that block the growing life-style of a church can be very difficult to overcome. But, all church growth problems can be identified, isolated, and overcome.

In the following chapter we will seek to identify some of the hindrances to church growth. Not all are listed. The use of words that can apply to every situation is impossible. These are common hindrances that will provide an umbrella under which many varieties may be discovered.

Addressing our message and strategy to a limited population is a hindrance to church growth.

Every person has the right to hear the gospel in his own language, culture, and tradition. Churches are limited by the number of language, cultural, and traditional barriers they can cross with one type of staff, building, strategy, location, and program. The limited capacities and resources of a church indicate all persons cannot be reached by one church.

To insist that persons respond to the gospel in the manner prescribed by a given church is to invite a limitation to growth.

Addressing the Message to a Limited Population

There are thousands of churches that are basically white, Anglo-Saxon, and Protestant in context and content (WASP). The people in these churches are a great deal alike regardless of where they are located geographically.

A majority of mainline Protestant denominations are basically "WASP-oid" in staff, building space, strategy, and program. Outreach or evangelism tracts, Bible study guides, Sunday by Sunday curriculum pieces, hymnbooks, and publicity materials are focused on this WASPoid segment of society. Thus, many WASPoid persons can move from place to place and usually find their particular "kind" of church.

According to one study 56.6 percent of the American population is "melted" or "American." [1] These have more or less adopted a basic "American life-style" and large numbers of them can assimilate into the WASP language, culture, and tradition. On the basis of presenting the gospel in and through WASPoid language, culture, and tradition millions of Americans can be reached for Christ and responsible church membership.

Even within the WASP culture there are many varieties of subcultures that are not exactly alike. In fact, in some instances the cultural distances involved may create a climate of incompatibility. This creates complex problems for church growth. The problems become more complex when these facts are ignored or considered unimportant.

A good case in point is as follows. A typical Southern WASP moves to a Northern industrial area. It is a large metropolitan situation. When the gospel is shared with these persons from a minister using other words, cultural nuances, and traditional illustrations, there are barriers to be overcome before the Southern WASP can receive the message. If the building in which the service is held in not customarily WASPoid in appearance, design, or location, other barriers come into being. When the Sunday bulletin or weekly paper reflects strategies and programs unfamiliar to this person, still other barriers present themselves.

What has happened in this case is the message and strategy has been addressed to a population that is not in the absolute center of what is considered WASP. Therefore, the WASPoid person will either overcome the barriers, go where the barriers are not present, or drop out of church life altogether and become indifferent to the cause of Christ.

This illustration only applies to the Southern WASP who is interested enough to seek out a place where he can hear a gospel message. The problem is more complex when we consider a Southern WASP who has no interest in hearing the gospel or in developing his spiritual life.

This illustration can be reversed when a native of the Northern section of America moves to a Southern city. His white, Anglo-Saxon, Protestant language, culture, and traditions may not mix with those of the South. He can be lost to Christ and the mission of the church because the message of the gospel as presented in the Southern church is too "Southern oriented" to meet him at his point of awareness.

A church can get so involved in reaching its "own kind" that hundreds of persons are unreached or overlooked. It is inaccurate to conclude that most communities are "melted." The gospel message abides but the language, culture, and tradition to which it applies varies.

A Limited Strategy Can Limit Church Growth

Efforts to increase church attendance by a regular visitation program is a proven, growth-producing activity. But, many churches are working at this harder and harder and accomplishing less and less. Large amounts of time are being spent visiting and fewer people are responding.

It is entirely possible the visitation program is focused on only one segment of the population in the community.

A church in a Northern city can focus its attention on Southerners who are transferred by their employers.

Pastors have been known to drive through parking lots in cities looking for cars with license plates from Southern states. He may leave notes or business cards encouraging church attendance.

Church leaders have been known to read newcomers' listings and select only those who move from Southern states as prospects for visitation.

Pastors may select three homes eight to thirteen miles apart and spend an entire afternoon driving by hundreds of homes to find three families that are "our kind of folks."

There is approximately 43.4 percent of the American population described as "unmelted." [2] This number is increasing. It is incorrect to assume all these people want to be assimilated into some variety of the WASP language, culture, and tradition. Nor do they want the message and strategy of the church to be addressed to them in WASPoid semantics or traditions.

Advertising efforts, youth programs, special emphasis services, social ministries, and financial endeavors must be considered in light of the unreached in the community who are some cultural distance from the message and strategy of the church.

A "WASPoid" person has difficulty crossing language, cultural and traditional barriers not familiar to him. The person who is not "WASPoid" also has difficulty crossing barriers when he comes from the opposite direction.

This is not a twentieth-century spiritual phenomenon. It is apparent in Acts 15:1–11 (NIV) that the Hebrew Christians had a theological struggle with the growth of the early church.

> Some men came down from Judea to Antioch and were teaching the brothers: "Unless you are circumcised according to the custom taught by Moses, you cannot be saved." This brought Paul and Barnabas into sharp dispute and debate with them. So Paul and Barnabas were appointed, along with some other believers, to go up to Jerusalem to see the apostles and elders about this question. . . .
>
> Then some of the believers who belonged to the party of the Pharisees stood up and said, "The Gentiles must be circumcised and required to obey the law of Moses."
>
> The apostles and elders met to consider this question. After much discussion, Peter got up and addressed them: "Brothers, you know that some time ago God made a choice among you that the Gentiles might hear from my lips the message of the gospel and believe. . . .
>
> We believe it is through the grace of our Lord Jesus that we are saved, just as they are."

They wanted to insist that every Gentile convert to Christianity be brought into the family of God through the Hebrew tradition, namely "circumcision." The Gentiles resisted this. What the Hebrew mind considered theological the Gentile mind considered cultural. The issue was never absolutely resolved.

The place of Jerusalem in the mind of the Hebrew was essential to the growth of the kingdom of God in the world. The Gentile mind considered the mission of world evangelization more important than the place of its beginning. So, the growth of the kingdom of God as represented by evangelical churches was actually launched from Antioch.

Twentieth-century churches must face realistically that all mind-sets are not alike, nor shall they ever be. Even as powerful as the gospel message is, it cannot break down every barrier and make us sociologically, theologically, traditionally, and linguistically one.

A church that addresses the gospel and growth strategies to only one "type" of person will ultimately limit its growth.

* Churches do this without being aware of it.
* Churches do it deliberately.
* Churches that want to grow face it and do all that is within their power to change their language, culture, and tradition to be more inclusive.

To share the gospel with only one strata of the population of a community is to open the door to nongrowth. To design strategies that are acceptable to only one segment of the population in a community is to present a hazard for church growth to overcome.

Spiritual problems within the church can limit growth.

A non-Christian value system is the signal of spiritual problems within the church. *When the "value system" of a large number of church members is based more on the non-Christian ethic than the Christian ethic, the church is likely to experience stagnation or decline.* Appetites of the flesh, governed by human nature rather than the Spirit of God, produce stunted growth in the church.

The key to changing the world through the work of a growing church is to reach people who come into the church by *conversion.* Significant coversion growth does not occur when church members neutralize the witness of the church by carnal behavior.

The use of human wisdom can be beneficial to church growth. But, when this wisdom takes precedence over seeking divine guidance, church growth can be seriously arrested. Ambition in church leaders is one of the great, untapped resources of the church in our day. But, this ambition must not grow out of natural, transient works of men which center on achievement at all costs.

The success-at-all-costs syndrome prevalent in today's society must be lovingly resisted by the church. Feeding people to a "statistic machine" is a death-producing activity to lasting church growth. Church leaders, with appetites for ego-centered success, must be challenged to rethink their motives. God wanted to grow a great church at Corinth. The church was to be built on his greatness and success (1 Cor. 1:23–24, NIV): "We preach Christ crucified: a stumbling block to Jews and foolishness to Gentiles, but to those whom God has called, both Jews and Greeks, Christ the power of God and the wisdom of God." Apollos, Paul, and Peter were secondary factors in the growth of that church. The truth of this illustration must be applied to the context of today.

Carnality can lead to a lack of emphasis on the lordship of Christ in the total life of every Christian. Carnality can be described as allowing the appetites of the flesh and attitudes of the flesh to be governed by human nature rather than the Spirit of God. This can produce stunted growth in a Christian and in the church. In all quantitatively and qualitatively growing churches, the lordship of Christ is a prevalent theme. Unless church members are called to maximum discipleship there will be a tendency to settle for minimum discipleship. Church leaders must be willing to commit to a life that is increasingly controlled by God. Nongrowing churches do not experience seeing young adults responding to a calling to the lordship of Christ with regards to vocations and careers. Their young people are not vibrant witnesses on the high school campuses. The adult members of a church will not make significant impact on a community if they are not led and nurtured to accept the lordship of Christ over all of life. To neglect this call to commitment is a pattern of carnal behavior.

Power groups within the church family can produce significant limitations to growth. Thousands of churches across America suffer from this carnal behavior. Many of them are described by a recent book, *The Seven Last Words of the Church, We Never Did It That Way Before.*[3] Crossing geographical, cultural, and racial barriers will never occur if a power struggle to prevent it is going on within the internal life of the church. A power group often resists growth in the church because it can lead to reaching those who are "not of *our* kind." An "exclusive" attitude in the church is a carnal attitude.

Unbelief Limits Church Growth

God-can't-do-that-here syndrome. This is not often a bold, forthright statement. It is usually a very subtle pattern of thinking. It is spoken in hushed tones among certain people in the church family. It can stifle church growth when it becomes a prevalent pattern of thought or conversation.

We can become so familiar with God that we limit his work in our specific situation. It is tragic how we can make God seem like an ordinary person restricted by ordinary limitations. This leads us to assume that church growth is all but impossible. We estimate the size of hazards to growth and assume they are greater than the resources of God. This leads to what Robert Schuller calls "impossibility thinking." [4] According to Schuller, growth goals can be made impossible in three ways:

(1) When you do nothing about them

(2) When you quit somewhere along the way

(3) When you accept failure as final

Not all unbelief is outside the Christian faith. Not all unbelief is displayed through a rejection of Christ. The people of God can let unbelief stifle growth within God's church. When we say, "God can't do that here," we are actually saying "God can't do that through us who are here." This is unbelief and it can seriously retard church growth wherever it prevails.

Unbelief can express itself in an unwillingness to risk. The faith dimension of the work of God does not come into focus until a church extends herself beyond her resources. This means attempting a task that appears at the outset to be impossible. Significant growth, whether quantitative or qualitative, must go beyond the unbelief dimension to the faith dimension. Risk is always a factor in church growth. Unbelievers tend to resist anything that may produce an unknown or uncontrollable experience.

Unbelief is never a private affair. It sets up a chain reaction of failures, neglect, apathy and missed opportunities. To approach church growth with unbelief is to thwart the work of God. In Matthew 13:55–58 (NIV) is the record of how unbelief can bring a negative effect on the work of God.

> "Isn't this the carpenter's son? Isn't his mother's name Mary, and aren't his brothers James, Joseph, Simon and Judas? Aren't all his sisters with us? Where then did this man get all these things?" And they took offense at him.
>
> But Jesus said to them, "Only in his home town and in his own house is a prophet without honor."
>
> And he did not do many miracles there because of their lack of faith.

God wants a church to grow. He wants it to grow in its inward life. He wants it to extend itself to all the peoples of the world. Unbelief can limit these facets of growth.

Crystallization of the Organization Limits Church Growth

Some church organizations are too much like their cornerstones: set in concrete. Church growth occurs best in a church were the needs of people precede the establishment of organizational patterns. Whether or not the needs of the people are being met should become the criterion by which the organization is judged.

Culture has had some seriously negative effects in this area of church life. We continue an organization because it was handed down as a worthy organization of the past. Often our culture, rather than our theology or strategy, dominates our thinking about present and future organizational patterns. When human needs take priority consideration, an organization must be alert and willing to change, because human needs change from time to time. Human needs are spontaneous, therefore, organizations to meet human need must be open to spontaneity and change.

To crystallize the organization so permanently that the church resists change opens one door to limiting church growth.

Frozen evaluation of the organization is a sign of crystallization of the organization.

One sure way to contribute to a crystallized and firmly established organization is to evaluate each facet of the organization the same way. Two extremes which result from change polarize around reaction and overreaction. Somewhere in between these extremes must be the arena of activity for the church that wants to grow in the environment of today.

Not all units of an organization have the same contribution to make to church growth.

1. Some organizational units are designed for inward growth.

2. Some organizational units are designed for outward growth.

3. Some organizational units are temporary while others are permanent.

Frozen evaluation leads to the neglect of these truths. Churches that want to grow need to adopt a procedure in which organizational units pass the "functional validity test" [5] before being allowed to continue. Some units need to be tested annually and others less frequently. The crucial question so frequently ignored concerning an organization unit is, "What purpose does this unit serve in the inward and/or outward growth of our church?"

A frozen evaluation that will not yield to the changing, realigning, or discontinuing of certain organizational units is contributing to a lack of growth in the church.

Another expression of crystallization of the organization is seen in resistance to new units.

An organization stays alive by adding new dimensions to its ongoing plans, strategies, and activities. The following give some idea of the new unit concept:

New people integrated into an organization bring growth

New units that enlarge the organization bring growth

New organizational units that offer a variety of ministries bring growth

New space in which the organization may function brings growth

New leadership in the organization can produce growth

These new units may not fit into old forms. This is true of people, departments, classes, ministries, or facilities.

It is astonishing how much resistance there is to the new unit concept. It may be expressed by deliberate, nonvisible efforts to neutralize plans for expansion. It may be a power struggle that is visible to the church family and the community.

New units grow faster when they are allowed to be indigenous. They are more adaptable to "need oriented" functioning. Their rapid growth often threatens the status quo. There is always the possibility they may create new varieties of ministry. From them may come a challenging question, "Why is this the way we have always done it?"

New units may bring in people who are not "like" the majority of the church family.

New units will bring new personal problems to be dealt with.

New units will bring new financial demands.

New units will contribute to the needs for reevaluation of the organization.

New units will create space problems.

New unit growth is the only area in which *significant church growth* will take place in the next twenty-five years.

To resist new unit growth is to seriously limit the growth of the church today and tomorrow.

Resistance to research is a sign of crystallization of the organization.

Most church growth measurement takes place by:

1. Counting the visible response to the call for church membership;
2. Assessing increase financial support; or
3. The memory of a church leader.

All too frequently the desire is lacking to really know how a given church is growing. There are methods and procedures that can provide adequate and accurate information on the growth profile of any church. But, the leaders in a church must really want to know the facts about the growth of their church. How is resistance to church growth research expressed?

1. By not caring to know the facts about church growth;

2. By an unwillingness to do the work necessary for gathering facts and figures that will give accurate information;

3. By considering self-study a nonspiritual work;

4. By neglecting to provide time priority for an adequate self-study.

It takes effort to prevent this statement from being descriptive of a church: "When people are wedded to a conclusion, there develops a state of mind which makes them blind to evidence that does not support the conclusion." [6]

Scientific analysis of church growth *can* be done. Instruments man has developed make it possible. The computer, the hand calculator, the study of charts and graphs are commonplace tools in the environment of our day. To consider these tools profane or insignificant is to resist some of the most helpful resources for accurately studying church growth.

A resistance to proper research is a definite limitation to church growth.

Planning Too Small Limits Church Growth

Shrinking plans to what human capacities and resources can carry out is planning too small. Leaving things as they are in order to avoid creating inconvenient situations is planning too small. Assuming the responsibility of a church is completed by having Sunday services is planning too small. Failure to look at the future of a church and what it shall be is planning too small. Allowing finances to become the predominant concern of a church is planning too small.

Plans must go beyond what can be accomplished without the help of God. The faith dimension of planning calls for risk, prayer, spontaneity, openness, and willingness to change. A sure and certain way to stifle church growth is to plan only what we are sure we can do with present resources.

No Plan at All Is Planning Too Small

Some churches do not plan at all. Whatever happens just happens and no definite course of action is followed. Tragically, these churches assume this is a plan in the faith dimension. God's plans are not based on chance happenings. His plans have always involved the people who make up his family. His plan for his people is generalized by Jesus in Matthew 16:18, "And I say also unto thee, That thou art Peter, and upon this rock I will build my church; and the gates of hell shall not prevail against it" (KJV). It is further detailed in Acts 1:8, "But ye shall receive power, after that the Holy Ghost is come upon you: and ye shall be witnesses unto me both in

Jerusalem, and in all Judaea, and in Samaria, and unto the uttermost part of the earth" (KJV). In Romans 12 and Ephesians 4:7–16 a careful strategy for the work of the family of God is shown. The church must plan to fit into this plan of God. This will not happen automatically. It requires a definite plan. An overemphasis on maintenance ministries does not lead to planning in the faith dimension. To get involved in the plan of God demands entering into the faith dimension.

Some church leaders fail to plan in the faith dimension because of fear.

Some church leaders fail to plan in the faith dimension because they lack knowledge of the promises of God for specific help to meet specific needs.

Some church leaders fail to plan in the faith dimension because they fail to count the resources of God among their assets.

Plans that do not enter the faith dimension seriously hamper church growth.

Overemphasis on Planning Maintenance Ministries

Maintenance ministries are those ministry units that exist because they always have or because they keep the church going on a week-by-week basis. These have very basic, important, and spiritual contributions to make to church growth. However, these can become the total program of the church. When the plan for maintaining the organization "as it is" consumes more time, resources, and personnel than expansion growth, that plan is too small. There must be a careful balance between maintenance and expansion growth. This can be done only by careful planning.

Maintenance ministries tend to neglect new unit growth within the present organization.

Maintenance ministries tend to neglect expansion growth beyond the present organization.

Maintenance ministries tend to neglect bridging growth beyond the present organization.

A study of most nongrowing churches will reveal that most of their plans center around a maintenance ministry. A plan to keep things as they have always been is a plan to impair growth.

Failure to Base Plans on Human Need Is to Plan Too Small

Human need is to be a prime motivator in the planning process. No plan for church growth can ignore discovering "people needs." A church cannot afford to operate on the assumption that it knows what is needed by every person. Plans constructed in isolation with no regard for the needs of people outside the church will not lead to significant new unit expansion or extension growth.

Far too often the nongrowing church has assumed it is enough to have an appropriately displayed sign in the front yard with church activities and the times of their occurrence. The expression has been made, "They know we're here; if they were really serious about spiritual things, they would come." The crucial question is, "What does the church plan that will create a desire for them to attend or even investigate?"

Some physical needs are too great to be met by Bible lessons and worship services.

Some emotional needs are too intimate to be dealt with in a large group setting.

Distrust of religious organizations cannot be overcome by merely forcing hostile people into yet another religious mold.

Loneliness is not cured by talking about it in committee meetings.

People who are lost from God and his plan for their lives must become the focal point of strategy planning. These plans must be large enough to include a variety of needs as well as meeting the need for a spiritual relationship to God. To neglect this enlarged planning is to encircle church growth with another limitation.

Allowing Finances to Determine the Plan Is to Plan Too Small

How many plans are still lying on the shelf of a church office because they became entangled in a cost analysis before they passed the *functional* and *need* tests?

It may be this is the most serious limitation to church growth. "God can't do that here because we can't pay for it."

The crucial question is: How does this plan contribute to church growth?

The crucial question is *not*: How much does it cost?

Thousands of churches are not growing today because these two questions have been reversed in the planning process.

The failure of organizational leaders to plan for costs is not advocated here. But an organization is crystallized when the most important and time-consuming activity on its agenda is cost analysis. The organization is trapped into planning too small. And, it has chosen to limit its growth.

The church is an organism with an organization natural to it. This organization cannot grow without cost. Church growth costs much more than money, but money is far too often the most serious concern in the planning process of a church.

When the priority of all planning is based on how much a plan costs, church growth is going to be seriously limited.

Strategies not Designed for Growth Limit Church Growth

Strategy is the method by which a plan is to be carried out.

Inadequate strategies are usually the results of inadequate planning. Right strategies usually surface when planning is properly done. Plans are the blueprints from which strategies are to be built.

Neglect of accurate research is an indication of a strategy not designed for growth.

Neglect of accurate research sets up a chain reaction. Poor research yields poor information to the planning process. Poor planning gives a poor foundation for strategy execution. Poor strategy execution leads to arrested, slow, or no growth.

Churches by the hundreds do not grow because they do not have a strategy for growth. The theological accuracy, fellowship, buildings, and leadership of a church may be above average. However, none nor all of these guarantee the church will grow significantly. Unless a church studies its past, present, and future, an adequate strategy for growth will be an "accident." Far too many are waiting for this "accident" to happen.

Churches often overlook facing the question, "How is our church growing?"

Is it experiencing *biological growth?* Biological growth should be defined as persons united with the church by baptism, who come from church-related families. This type growth is a fundamental responsibility of the church. But, this type growth alone will not create a dynamic church-growth program. To depend solely on this type growth is to invite spiritual decline and stagnation.

Is it experiencing *transfer growth?* Transfer growth is defined as persons uniting with the church by moving their membership from one church to another. These are already professing Christians before they unite with the church. (These may come into the church by baptism.) The normal procedure would be for these to unite with the church by requesting a letter of commendation from a previous church.

Is it experiencing *conversion growth?* Conversion growth is defined as persons uniting with the church by baptism. These would be persons who come from outside the church-related family. They are new to the ideas, programs, and doctrines of the church. They are converted from the world.

A church can have numerous experiences of biological growth and still not significantly affect the nonchurched people of the community . Those reached through biological growth are already predisposed to spiritual things. They do not represent a large majority of the unchurched population in America today.

A church can have many experiences of transfer growth. These will influence the unchurched of the community more than biological growth. These, too, are somewhat predisposed to spiritual things. They are more representative of the unchurched population but are also predisposed to spiritual things.

The most significant growth of the church is in the conversion growth dimension. This growth adds to the kingdom of God. It opens new unit expansion possibilities and can change the community and the world. This group represents the need of millions of people today.

When the question, "How is our church growing?" is neglected, inadequate planning is the result. When the plans miss the mark, the strategy will soon follow the same pattern. Carefully planned strategies are crucial to a balanced program of growth in the church. Neglecting the study that shows a need for this balance places a limitation on church growth.

A failure to recognize responsive areas leads to inadequate strategies.

Not all areas of a community are equally responsive to the gospel at one given time. To assume methods of communicating with the spiritually interested and spiritually disinterested are the same is the wrong assumption.

Responsive units of people in a given section of a community should receive priority attention. It should not be deemed more spiritually noble to continue pouring resources into nonresponsive areas to the neglect of responsive areas. Churches do this all too frequently. Personnel, time, and finances are not available to take advantage of a new, responsive area because these resources have been allocated to nonresponsive area. Spiritual need is often very spontaneous. Some strategy must take into account that all persons will not respond at the same time interval.

When a church finds itself so overly committed to nonresponsive areas that it cannot consider meeting the needs in responsive areas, it has an inadequate strategy.

Misuse of Time, Energy, and Gifts Is an Inadequate Strategy for Growth

The wasting time habit is an inadequate strategy.

A study of minute by minute use of time by many committees, boards, or task forces of a church will reveal some interesting facts about how time is being used.[7]

When groups of people meet to consider church matters, how much time is spent in planning for growth? A time use analysis will startle the average leader who will investigate it. Over the period of a year hundreds of people hours are wasted on nongrowth thinking. Deacon groups often leave the ministering to human need for conducting business affairs within the church. Pastors are often snared by the same trap. Finance committees assume *maintenance* budget planning is more important than any other. "Dream" or "Faith" budgets rarely receive priority time or attention from a finance committee.

Many of the things to which time is given are important and necessary. But, when church growth is needed, a rearrangement of time use is essential. Maximum time must be spent in praying and planning for church growth.

There is only a selected amount of time that lay persons can share with their church. If growth is a major goal of that church, then time must be given to growth thinking and planning.

Pastors and other church leaders can find their time being spent on a multitude of demands. When the leader of the church finds his schedule is overcrowded, time spent in thinking about and planning for church growth is too often the first area of neglect.

Persons who have the mind and will to grow should be allowed to spend their time on growth-oriented items. To overlook this is to invite yet another limitation to hinder church growth.

The wasting energy habit is an inadequate strategy.

The first eight months in the Christian experience of a new convert can be one of the most growth producing time periods in his or her life. The new Christian going to his associates and loved ones with the fresh fervor of the new birth experience is one of the most powerful forces for church growth. All too frequently, this new convert becomes so involved in the church that his best energies are used in maintaining what is already in existence in the church.

Peter Wagner forwards the idea that only 10 percent of all church members can be door-to-door evangelists. The rest are more comfortable with cultivative evangelism. It is obvious many of these 10 percent are using their energies to nail shingles on the church roof, assist in maintaining the church lawn, or serving on committees that are oriented to maintaining the church "as is."

As in the use of time, there must be a concerted effort to properly use the energies of church members. Physical limitations are a reality to every person. Church growth thinking and planning can end up as the last item on the agenda of a meeting that lasts from 7:30 P.M. to 9:30 P.M. Pastors, housewives, and businessmen are not at their best at 9:30 P.M. Great thinking and planning are not fruits of fatigue. It is a waste of valuable energy to give the best of ourselves to everything else and then discuss growth problems and needs.

Any church with a serious desire to grow *must* use human energy when it is at its peak. To exhaust people with programs at the church and expect them to be outreach minded while in a state of fatigue is not a wise use of energy.

Training of church members to use their gifts to contribute to the life of the church is a must in the church that wants to grow. Neglect of church member development will result in a tragic waste of talent. Trained workmen for the Master have a way of being used by him to expand the kingdom of God. It is a basic principle of the Word of God that one gives what he has to God and God multiplies it and produces fruit from it. Christ spent three years giving intensive training to twelve believers. And, God, through them, changed the world.

There are thousands of church members sitting as spectators who might be participants in church growth if the call for their gifts were sounded. The church that does not sound that call is wasting valuable talent that could break down many limitations to church growth.

Often apathy is mistaken for undermotivation. A growth-minded leader or lay person may have little or no interest in keeping everything as it has always been. But, being challenged with new growth possibilities, both personally and corporately, may stimulate an entirely different response. There are undermotivated persons in every church awaiting the stimulus of a new challenge. To assume this is not true provides a hazard to growth in the church.

The wasting gifts habit is an inadequate strategy.

Undermotivation could well be the major cause for lack of participation in church growth. Undermotivation may result from a Christian's not being used to do what he or she does best. Gifts have been given by God to individual Christians everywhere.

Some of us have been given special ability as apostles; to others he has given the gift of being able to preach well; some have special ability in winning people to Christ, helping them to trust him as their Savior; still others have a gift for caring for God's people as a shepherd does his sheep, leading and teaching them in the ways of God.

Why is it that he gives us these special abilities to do certain things best? It is that God's people will be equipped to do better work for him, building up the church, the body of Christ, to a position of strength and maturity (Eph. 4:11–12, TLB).

These gifts are to be used. The church has a responsibility for finding avenues through which these gifts can be expressed. These avenues are not found by accident. They are found by purposeful planning. Entire denominations can suffer from the neglect of the gifts of the believers. Certain activities can be so rigidly followed by a denomination that any young leader who cannot perform accordingly has no place of service made available to him or her. Churches can suffer from the same pattern of conduct. Not every person has the same talent or gift to share with the church. But the church that wants to reach out to all people must find ways for all people who are reached to make a contribution to the inward and outward growth of the church.

The Failure to Decide to Grow Limits Church Growth

Indecision can be disastrous. This is especially true with regard to church growth. Church growth always begins with someone *deciding* it is time to do something.

It is inaccurate to assume that all churches want to grow. Some do not. Some are quite indifferent about growing or not growing. The only way to escape this snare is by an act of the will. The will influences every decision in life. A church can have a corporate will. This corporate will influences every decision the church makes.

Being sincere will not guarantee church growth.

Being theologically accurate will not guarantee church growth.

Having a trained minister or group of trained ministers will not guarantee church growth.

Building an adequate and beautiful building will not guarantee church growth.

Studying accurate research about the church will not guarantee church growth.

There are thousands of churches with all these assets, but they are not growing. One primary reason is found in the fact they have failed to decide to grow. They have neglected to willfully say: "God wants every church to grow, and if this is the will of God, we must make it our will too!"

All problems cannot be solved with this one decision. But, the most difficult problem is solved. The decision to grow creates a mind-set. Growth becomes a priority. Growth becomes a way of life. Growth is expected. This decision is the one that opens the door to all the resources available for church growth. This one decision can break down many of the limitations discussed in the previous pages.

It is a tragic truth to face, but many churches have yet to decide to grow. They have chosen the limitations when they could have chosen limitless possibilities for growing through expansion and extension. "Whenever people start thinking in achievement oriented terms, things start to happen." [8]

3
Principles of Church Growth

Webster has defined principle as, "a fundamental truth; a primary or basic law, doctrine, or the like." [1] That is the definition for the word principle in the title of this chapter. The emphasis in this chapter will be placed on the phrase "a fundamental truth."

Church growth is an indigenous affair. A church must grow up in a place and fashion its ministry in such a way that it is natural to the community. What creates church growth in one geographical and social setting may or may not produce the same results in another.

A fundamental truth used in different locations may have to be applied in a different manner, use different words, involve different time frames, and use different types of leaders. Churches have personalities and some methods will not work with certain types of personalities. The principle or fundamental truth supporting the method may be biblically sound, theologically accurate, and work magnificently somewhere else. But, if it fails to be viewed as indigenous to the local situation to which it is applied, it will not produce growth.

The principles mentioned in this chapter are limited in scope by the language used to express them. No use of words can be universally precise.

These principles are at work in churches throughout America. Some of the churches are very small and some very large. Others lie between these two extremes.

These principles must be considered as part of a mixture of factors that can create a climate for church growth, launch a church into growth, and maintain growth as a continuous life-style in a church.

It is a basic premise of this book that every church can and should grow. And, church growth principles apply in some way to every situation.

Principle of the Bible Study Priority

It was said of the early church at its beginning: "They spent their time

45

in learning from the apostles, taking part in the fellowship (Acts 2:42, TEV). Within a short period of time a new problem arose. The leaders of that infant church were being called on to perform a fragmented ministry that led away from this priority.

"It is not right for us to neglect the preaching of God's word in order to handle finances. So then, brothers, choose seven men among you who are known to be full of the Holy Spirit and wisdom, and we will put them in charge of this matter. We ourselves, then, will give our full time to prayer and the work of preaching."

So the word of God continued to spread. The number of disciples in Jerusalem grew larger and larger (Acts 6:2–4,7, TEV).

Bible study must be more than Sunday School.

Sunday School generally takes place on Sunday morning prior to or following a corporate worship service. Many major denominations consider this Sunday morning Bible study time as the key program of the church. It has played an essential role in the life of churches for years.

Southern Baptist have viewed Sunday School as the building block of church growth and development since their beginning in 1845. The early Sunday School programs of Southern Baptists were not so refined as those they have now. But, Bible study through a Sunday School medium has been foundational for them for over a century. Southern Baptist leaders have been known to say "we reach for baptism and church membership two out of four unchurched people who will attend our Sunday School for six months, and we reach one out of two hundred for baptism and church membership who attend only the morning worship service for this period of time."

There are large, independent or nondenominational churches that have built their strength through a heavy emphasis on Sunday School.

But, Sunday School alone is not enough. An overview of potential or real problems must be considered.

* The problem arises for these groups when this attendance begins to show an arrested growth profile or a declining one. Southern Baptist have not shown a substantial annual gain in Sunday School enrollment since 1954. This has affected every enrollment figure in the church. It has substantially influenced their baptismal and conversion growth rate. But, it is interesting to note the financial contribution growth in Southern Baptist life has shown substantial increase through the same period of time.

* Still another problem arises when the Sunday School becomes an

end in itself rather than a means to an end, namely, total church growth. Sunday School leaders can lose the focus of the Sunday School as an outreach organization that is to lead persons to Christ and meaningful church membership.

* A problem surfaces when space for Sunday School departments and classes cannot be built rapidly enough to leave room for growth. Bus ministries utilized for Sunday School growth can contribute to this problem. Aggressive outreach or growth oriented Sunday School leaders and/or pastors can also bring this about.

* The vocational life of Americans is no longer limited to Monday— Saturday as work days with Sunday free. Thousands of persons are overlooked because of their inability to be "at the church" on Sunday morning.

* Total fellowship needs cannot be met through the Sunday School program alone. Bible study and fellowship are shown as companions in the New Testament. Regardless of how efficiently the forty to forty-five minutes are used on Sunday morning, the need for fellowship along with Bible study cannot be met.

* Sunday School is too often focused on a church school for children. Ken Chafin, once said, "The Bible is an adult book." Many view Sunday School as a place where sweet, little Bible stories are taught. This is especially true of unchurched people. It really does not matter that it is not true. The fact is, they perceive Sunday School this way and no casual efforts will change their point of view.

Study of the Word of God is too integral a part of church growth to be organized for Sunday morning only. The issue churches are facing is a need for more opportunity for Bible study for members and nonmembers.

It is incorrect to assume people are not interested in Bible study when they do not attend Sunday School. It may be their response is more directed towards the time of day, the setting, the quality of teaching, the curriculum used, or the quality of acceptance.

If the gospel is as good as we say it is, *and it is,* then we must give priority to a strategy that will allow it to be presented to more people, in more places, in more types of situations, and more often than Sunday morning.

Bible study groups are surfacing all over America. No denomination has all their Bible study groups organized. Many people are seeking a word from God for their lives. What they do not find on Sunday morning at the church they are seeking elsewhere through the week.

These groups are meeting in homes, shops, factories, offices, coffee shops, schools, athletic dorms, locker rooms in stadiums, medical clinics, and a myriad of other types of locations.

These Bible study groups are not to be viewed as an adversary to Sunday School. They are allies. Sunday School cannot meet the total Bible study needs among the churched or unchurched peoples. Obviously there will be some of these groups that create disturbances within the church. But, the truth is, they already are creating disturbances, it is just not so public as a singular group can make it seem.

The risk of thousands of Bible study groups, with no organizational control, inadequate educators as teachers, materials that may not be theologically pure is a true risk. It is not a figment of the imagination.

But, the alternative is not lethargy, rejection, business as usual, or withdrawal of fellowship. Bible study is the foundational function of reaching people for Christ and responsible church membership.

* Creative strategies to get the Word into more lives is a crucial building block for church growth.

* Designs for creating Bible studies that are built around fellowship with Christ and one another are essential to church growth.

* Training teachers to be skilled in leading Bible studies in nonorganized settings is a critical need in the growing church.

* Growing churches place heavy emphasis on Bible study inside and outside the church building.

* Nongrowing churches should consult their Bible study priorities. If all the emphasis is on Sunday School, this is not enough.

Bible study must be more than sharing biblical information.

Our Southern Baptist friends have a profound concept in one of their purpose statements for the Bible teaching program: "Teach the Biblical Revelation" [2]

Bible study is not centered around expounding historical information. Laymen do not delight in spending three nights of a five-night Bible study on the arguments of whether or not John the apostle wrote the Gospel of John and the Epistles.

Bible study that attracts unchurched people is not focused on the exact location of the showdown between David and Goliath. Nor do they find satisfaction in knowing the exact number of cubits taller Goliath was than David. Their interest is not in why David selected more than one rock from the brook. Their interest may pursue why David cut off the head of Goliath. But, their primary concern is, "What does this mean for me in my struggles today?" "What does the Bible reveal to us through its teaching that can equip us for the issues of vocational life, family life, church life, and personal life?" These are questions every Bible student has a right to ask.

Curriculum design is a crucial issue in denominations of our day. Churches must have Bible study materials that go beyond dispensing Bible data and facts. Social issues must be dealt with in the radical terms suggested by the Word of God. Daily problems must be faced realistically. Vocational decisions must be undergirded by guidance from the Word of God. Meaning for life must be declared as it is revealed in God's Word. Help for the lonely, the terminally ill, the seeming failures, the poor, discouraged, the ambitious, and the hopeless must be shared from the teaching of the revelation of the Word of God to people.

Growing churches do more than pass out helpful information from God's Word. The Bible has the ability to reveal truth to any individual who will study it.

Bible study can produce spiritually and intellectually growing people.

How people grow largely depends on what they eat. This is a biological and a spiritual truth. The Word of God does not diminish the capacity of a person to grow.

People grow when they read the promises of God in His Word and seek to live them out in their lives. "I can do all things in him who stengthens me" (Phil. 4:13, RSV).

People grow when they learn from the Word of God to pray and look for answered prayer. "Therefore I tell you, whatever you ask in prayer, believe that you receive it, and you will" (Mark 11:24, RSV).

People grow in stability when they find guidance and security in the Word of God. "Everyone then who hears these words of mine and does them will be like a wise man who built his house upon the rock; and the rain fell, and the floods came, and the winds blew and beat upon that house, but it did not fall, because it had been founded on the rock" (Matt. 7:24–25, RSV).

People can grow from hopeless sinners to forgiven sinners filled with hope. They can go from timid, shy, reticient witnesses to fearless, tastefully bold, radiant witnesses of the Christian faith. When one grows spiritually and bases that growth on spiritual truth, he frees his intellectual abilities to expand well beyond what is assumed by most observers.

The question may be surfacing, "What is so important about a Bible study that produces growing people?"

The answer lies in the fact we are studying principles of church growth. A key factor in church growth is to establish a Bible-study priority. A Bible study that produces growing people is an essential work of the Bible-study program in a growing church. And, growing churches are made up of growing people. Growing people attract people who want to grow.

The nongrowing church in America should take a careful look at the position Bible study holds in its calendar planning, financial expenditures, training emphases, and publicity.

Growing evangelical churches across America today have Bible study as a priority in profession and practice.

The Principle of Leadership

A leader is defined as:
(1) One who walks ahead of the groups;
(2) Keeps in advance without being too detached;
(3) Influences followers and moves them toward goals.

There are five classes of church leaders.

There is a leadership crisis in the church today. Churches determined to grow must meet and respond to this crisis. Donald McGavran and Wyn Arn have rightly surmised there are five classes or types of leaders within the church.

Types of Leaders [3]

CLASS I carries on the maintenance ministry of the church.

CLASS II are volunteer workers who head out away from the church.

CLASS III are leaders of small churches paid or partially paid.

CLASS IV are the paid, professional leaders of large or well-established congregations.

CLASS V travel from one country to another, know two or three languages and are part of the world church.

Class I leaders are significant factors in church growth.

These leaders maintain existing programs within the organizational structures of the churches. They spend the major portion of their time touching the lives of those who already have a relationship with Jesus Christ and are functioning within the church. These people sing in choirs, chair committees, maintain properties, hold office in mission organizations, assist in the worship services, and generally maintain what is in existence. Today's churches cannot function without a good working force of Class I leaders. To neglect this support group is to invite failure and thwart the growth efforts of a church.

Maintenance, or Class I leaders, can maintain growth awareness, growth concern and a "growth mind-set." Warmhearted Class I leaders respond positively to "new unit" thinking. They will encourage Class I leaders to reach out and bring new people and new thinking to the church.

The Class I corps of leaders provides the finest resource for Class II leaders. There are some leaders who can function as Class I and Class II leaders simultaneously. Usually, when priorities are selected by the Class I leaders, maintenance duties prevail.

Some people are functioning as Class I leaders because they have never been motivated to participate in growth activities as priorities. *Growing churches keep a "growth consciousness" before Class I leaders.*

It is obvious in the book of Acts many believers were involved in maintaining a strong base of operation to which people returned from time to time. They prayed, distributed the possessions that had been shared in common, deliberated over doctrinal issues, and cared for the widowed and the children who were left without parents. Maintenance leaders have always had a major function in the church of Jesus Christ.

Class II leaders are significant factors in church growth.

These leaders in a church seem to be able to relate with persons outside the church family. In fact, they like being involved with outreach activities that are not maintenance oriented.

These people know unreached people. They purposefully maintain contact with them. This type leader may tend to have limited concern for meetings at the church.

Growing churches utilize these outreach-minded people. Care must be taken to avoid giving maintenance responsibilities to these who have interests in growth through outreach. Churches can involve gifted Class II workers to the point that time and energy are expended primarily on nongrowth activities.

The Class II leader looks for ways to reach new people. He will cross all kinds of barriers to draw new people into a meaningful relationship with Jesus Christ and responsible church membership.

The Class II leader knows measurable and nonmeasurable growth must be kept in balance if a church is to maintain a healthy growth profile. However, he usually places more emphasis on measurable or quantitative growth.

When a church begins to experience arrested growth or decline over a period of time, an imbalance in leadership style can usually be found. The church will usually discover an overabundance of Class I leaders and too few Class II leaders.

There are many factors involved in outreach work. Many leaders are gifted at drawing people to church.

Some have the gift to lead nonbelievers to Jesus Christ. This is described in Ephesians 4:11 "Some have special ability in winning people to Christ, helping them to trust him as their Savior" (TLB).

Others know how to use small share groups and Bible study groups to reach out into the nonbelieving segments of the population. High school or college age youth are the focus of some.

Single adults receive the attention of others.

Senior citizens are the target group of other Class II leaders.

Class II leaders have what Donald McGavran calls "church growth eyes." They are always alert to new people. They look for opportunities or strategies that result in numerical growth.

Class III leaders are significant factors in church growth.

Class III leaders are leaders of smaller churches and may be totally or partially sustained financially by these churches. Most denominations that have clergy-led congregations will have a large number of these leaders. These represent the largest group of salaried or partially salaried leaders of most major denominations. Many times they will determine the growth pattern of a church for many years. If large numbers of these leaders are basically maintenance ministry oriented, it will significantly affect the type of growth within a denomination. This leader will greatly influence the growth "mind-set" of a church because he deals with small groups and is their recognized leader.

When these leaders assume growth as a priority for the church, there is a significantly measurable result. They can move small numbers of people towards goals. The larger a church becomes, the less one man can influence that church in a direct manner.

Class III leaders may be members of a large staff of a well-established church. They may be financially supported through a stipend. However, their total income is not dependent on the church in which they serve. When the Class III leader functions properly he will see that a major portion of his time should be spent working with Class I and II leaders moving them towards growth goals. His major time investment should be in this area of work.

Class IV leaders are significant factors in church growth.

Class IV leaders of churches represent the second largest salaried or partially salaried group. They receive their livelihood almost totally from a given constituency. Their role as motivators can never be overestimated. Through the help of others they can move large numbers of people toward growth goals.

Now, if Class III and Class IV leaders turn their energies towards growth as a priority, their churches *grow*. They grow significantly. It is a basic principle of church growth, "as go the leaders, so goes the church." Growing churches are led by growing leaders. No church grows beyond the point its leaders desire it to grow. Growing leaders attract growing followers. When the church leaders and their followers establish growth as a priority, the church grows.

Class IV leaders have extremely significant responsibilities. One major responsibility is the care, training, leading, inspiring, and motivation of Class I and Class II workers. These Class IV leaders are supposed to be "equippers." An equipper is one whose role is to furnish training and materials, and motivation for a particular service. The giving out of information is not the sum total of the responsibility of this equipper. He must study how to develop skill among volunteer leaders in maintenance and growth processes. This cannot be done in and through the preaching ministry alone. Training and materials are an integral part of the role of the equipper.

The principle of laity is a basic principle of church growth.

Unless it is an extremely unusual church, 99 percent of the congregation will be "nonclergy." The laity in this context is that group of people other than the pastoral leader who is salaried or partially salaried by the church.

Most growing churches have a strong, dynamic, aggressive pastor as a leader. He is usually a very gifted speaker or proclaimer of the message of God. Always, he is a motivator of people and can move a church toward growth priorities.

Growing churches must have men in the role of salaried leaders who can delegate the work responsibility. This delegation cannot be limited to the other staff members. No church can grow beyond the ability of the pastoral leader to delegate responsibilities to staff and lay ministers. To involve members in the growth of the church is not a strategy with which the Bible disagrees. Some are endowed with the gift to be pastoral leaders (Eph. 4:11, RSV). "And some pastors and teachers." We can describe them as pastoral ministers. The role of the pastor is one of an enabler or equipper—not merely a weekly proclaimer. Proclamation is only one function of the pastoral leader of the church.

Proclamation by one man eliminates the participation of 99 percent of the members of a given church. Follow the thought of this next diagram.

The *pastor* is the central figure in this religious function. *God* is to the side as a PROMPTER, ENABLER OR EQUIPPER giving the message and the strength of deliverance to the pastor. The observers are the

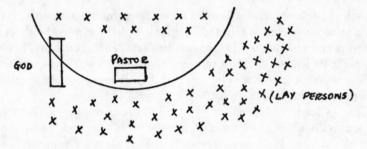

members of the congregation. Only a few of the lay persons are involved in the choir.

For the worship experience perhaps this is a suitable plan. There are certainly other alternatives. Surely one man is not the only person in the entire church family to receive a message that others need to hear.

However, the point is, this diagram becomes the pattern of far too many of all the church activities. We must face realities, a pastor is not equally gifted in *all* areas of the work of a church.

Growing churches may not use the following diagram as a guide but it is in substance descriptive of their pattern of strategy.

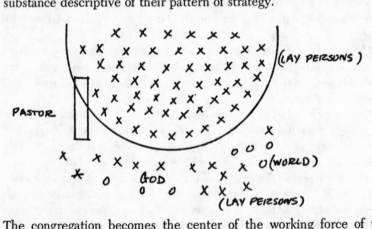

The congregation becomes the center of the working force of the growing church. They proclaim by showing what God is doing in and through their lives.

The pastor becomes the prompter, enabler or equipper. God observes, praises, offers help, and seeks to involve himself with the pastor and congregation simultaneously. The world in general serves as an observer of the experiences, sharing, and testimonies of the people of God.

There is a basic law in the universe summed up in "stimulus and response." The more stimuli present the more possible varieties of responses. The more personalities enriched by the presence of God that are displayed to the world, the more response may come from the world.

Lay ministers must become a mobilized force in the church if significant growth is to occur. In growing churches today there are always responsibilities for those with special gifts.

Special tasks within the growth program may necessitate the creation of new positions of service. Growing churches find arenas of service for its people. They make it *easy* for lay persons to be involved and feel needed.

The pastor in a growing church is always a central figure, but he is careful to surround himself with gifted, responsible, work-oriented lay persons who function as lay ministers.

The principle of a growth atmosphere is basic to church growth.

In a Growth Atmosphere People—Think Grow. Social activities, athletic activities, daily contacts, meetings of all types, and worship services are permeated by a growth mind-set in a growing church. In one church it was observed, "Even the custodians in this church talk about outreach growth." Growth is more than a project, it is a way of thinking and living.

> In growing churches people come together expecting something good to happen.
>
> In growing churches the accent is on the positive way of thinking and living.
>
> In growing churches every good idea receives a good hearing.
>
> In growing churches money is not the primary consideration. *People needs are!*
>
> In growing churches members enjoy serving.
>
> In growing churches the organizational structure is only a means to an end, not an end in itself.
>
> In growing churches the atmosphere of growth permeates every plan, strategy and activity.

In a growth atmosphere efforts are made to put people at ease.

Dentists have been working for years to make visits to them as non-threatening as possible. At times it appears churches have tried to reverse this procedure. Too often it is considered a mark of spiritual sincerity to make church attendance as threatening and painful as possible. The negative evaluation of the church from outsiders is often based on problems the church could solve with some effort.

Pleasant surroundings, inspiration, words of encouragement, Bible lessons and sermons focused at life needs, adequate nurseries, and surplus parking places, tend to contribute to placing people at ease with regards to church attendance and participation.

Response to the invitation to accept Christ, join the church, or renew Christian dedication should be as clear, warm, and personal as possible.

Growing churches respect the wants and needs of those they are reaching or trying to reach. A church that wants to grow must make the first time attendance experience as pleasant as possible.

Tensions and anxiety are not the fruits of new life in Christ.

Building up pressure for decision is not the way of the Spirit of God.

God always does his work in good taste with careful regard for the person with whom he is working. Growing churches follow this example as a basic principle of operation.

In a growth atmosphere there is time awareness.

Growing churches know the best time to do certain things. These churches tend to have a keen sense of timing. Churches have personalities just as people have personalities. There tends to be an ebb and flow.

There is another sense of time awareness. Growing churches know the time of their members is limited. Growing churches avoid wasting this time on nonessentials.

Growing churches must learn to make fewer permanent committees and more task forces which are temporary.

The leaders of growing churches consider talking with and witnessing to the unreached as having priority demand on their time.

In a growth atmosphere there is emphasis on a service image.

Growing churches consider themselves as service-oriented. They are aware their only reason for existence is to be of service to God and people.

The gifts of the members are used to be of service to God and others in growing churches.

Growing churches promote an image of "We're here to serve you" to all who come to their services.

Growing churches do not give the impression they are doing the community a favor by being present in the community.

Growing churches will inconvenience members in order to make it easier for nonmembers to attend or participate.

Growing churches prepare choirs, Bible study leaders, ushers, and members to be of service to the guests who attend.

Growing churches are conscious of giving an answer to the question Robert Schuller asks, "Who are we trying to impress?"

In hundreds of growing churches these principles may operate under a variety of names, plans, strategies, and actions. Put into operation, a growth atmosphere can create a climate for significant changes in the growth pattern of any size church.

The principle of small groups is a basic principle of church growth.

Any organism that lives is made up of cells. The church is a living organism. In the New Testament it is frequently referred to as a "body." It, too, is made up of cells. These cells are made of people from varying backgrounds, with a variety of personality traits, involved in a variety of vocational pursuits, made up of infinite physical and emotional variations, and varying quantities and qualities of energy capacities. But, they have a common bond that gives them the capacity to mold into the cell life— "The forgiveness of sin." We all come together from a background with one common ingredient—"imperfection."

A characteristic of any living organism is that it grows by cell division and cell multiplication. Churches grow as the members of small units within the church contribute to the growth and development of each person in the group.

Congregational worship experiences will not be sufficient nourishment for all the growing members of God's family. Small groups are essential for meeting the individual needs of the church family of today.

Gift discovery, development, and expression are best found in the small or cell group setting. Church growth can only occur when those individuals making up the "body" are growing individuals. Small groups within the church structure are essential for adequate, individual growth. Growing individual parts produce growing cells. Growing cells produce growing organisms made up of individual parts.

Church growth is often considered in a linear fashion of adding people. They who are added are farther and farther from the nucleus of the cell life of the church. An illustration might help . . .

Example of Linear Growth: The nucleus starts out with an x and o.

The nucleus starts adding x's to the (x) element of the nucleus.

Example: x + x + x + x

The nucleus also adds o's to the (o) element of the nucleus.

Example: o + o + o + o

The growth pattern could look like this:

x + x + x + xo + o + o + o

They who are added, whether they be (x) or (o), become farther and farther from the nucleus and from each other.

Example of Cell Growth: The nucleus starts out with an (x) and an (o).

(x) and (o) join to form (xo).

When additions are made to the nucleus it's growth pattern could look like this

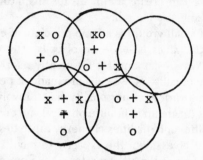

This appears to be the growth principle expressed in Acts 2:44–47. They began to share life qualities with each other. A meaningful sense of belonging to each other was a basic reality. Numerical enlargement meant an enlargement of spheres of relationships.

Organisms in biology grow in a sequence described as:

Metabolism: This is the stirring up and releasing of energy. A living organism is constantly doing both.

Growth: The organism expands from a beginning phase to a maturity phase.

Reproduction: The organism re-creates itself as a natural process.

Irritability: The organism responds to stimuli within that cause it to stir itself up and may result in destruction or releasing of new energy and the process begins anew.

Now, the church is an organism. It has the capacity to stir itself and release energy. The church can grow from an infancy or primitive beginning to maturity. A church is designed to reproduce itself in the world. It is a natural experience for the church to undergo times of inconvenience, negativism, and irritability.

This sequence of growth is lived out in small cell groupings within the church. The existence of these small groups may be recognized formally or they may exist informally, but they have existed, do exist, and will continue to exist. A basic principle to growth is to recognize their existence and utilize them to produce growth within the body known as the church.

Cell groups within the church have been known to have serious, negative impact on the body. They cannot be absolutely controlled. But, to ignore the reality of these groups is to ignore a basic law of nature and society.

Skill in utilizing these groups and placing an emphasis on guiding them will be more realistic than controlling them. In America today the small-group movement has just begun to have impact. The church that wants to grow should consider this reality. A definite plan for developing and utilizing small groups is essential to church growth.

Biological studies reveal that all living organisms are developed from a core substance in life called DNA.[4]

As part of the growth process a phase that grows from the activity of DNA is called chromosome development. Chromosomes go through a selection process that determines hereditary factors such as color of hair, eyes, skin color, and so on. This chromosome shops around until it matches with another chromosome and the selection is made and this chromosome feels at home and does the hereditary work that is natural to it.

A new person attends church. He shops around within the church until he finds a group with which he can identify. When he finds that group with which he feels at home, he joins.

Surveys are available which substantiate the fact that few people select, attend, and join a church because of the membership or theology of that church. People tend to find a group in that church with which they can identify. Once this discovery is made, they, like the chromosomes feel they have found a match. And, they join the relationship and fellowship of a small group. The closer a person feels to this group, the more naturally he can function effectively in the church.

Skill development in motivating, training, and utilizing small groups is a top priority in the growing church today.

The principle of evaluation and change is a basic principle of church growth.

Evaluation and change are companions. Careful evaluation will usually result in the discovery that something needs to be done differently.

Facing tough questions concerning the past, present, and future is crucial in church growth.

Growing churches must question the functional value of activities, organizational units, practices, and facilities. It is not easy to face a hard line of questioning about what has been, is, and shall be done.

A priority activity of church leaders must be to study what has been and is happening in the life of their church. For instance: If there is an imbalance of biological or transfer (95 percent) and only (5 percent) conversion growth, there must be a strategy change or the church will not make a significant spiritual impact on the community. This type of growth will eventually lead to stagnation and decline.

Another illustration:

A church decides it wants to grow. The goal for growth is a net increase of 300 in three years. Some crucial questions must be asked:

(1) Where will we park their cars?

(2) Where will we put them in our present building? Will we need more building space?

(3) What organizational changes will be necessary to serve the spiritual needs of these people?

(4) How large will the staff (paid and unpaid) of the church need to be to meet these peoples' needs? What staff changes will be needed?

These are only a few of the questions that must be faced. They are not "secular" questions as over against more "sacred" ones. They are absolutely essential to church growth.

Growing churches are not afraid to ask these questions. They respond to rather than react to these questions. Stimulation from finding a definite answer to a difficult question can motivate church leaders to new and innovative ways of doing the work of the church. Often the only reason a plan for growth does not work is the result of an inadequate strategy for carrying it out. The right questions may cause this to come to light.

When evaluation procedures are conducted, needed adjustments come into focus. This brings our thoughts to a continuing reality in the growing church—CHANGE!

Change is a way of life in church growth.

We are prone to forget that change is not a one-time experience. Change is a way of life. It is not an option. The only questions concerning change are: How much change and at what speed will it occur?

The growing church is a changing church.

Lyle Schuller has set out a strategy for change.[5]

Schaller 58

(1) A perceived crisis stimulates the need for change.

(2) An increasing level of discontent with the status quo.

(3) Increase the attractiveness of the proposed goal.

(4) Increase the number and frequency of discussions about the proposed course of action.

(5) Focus on building up the trust level in personal relationships rather than on the proposed change.

(6) Minimize precedent, tradition, and custom and start with as few encumbrances from the past as possible.

Those who want to lead and participate in the life of a growing church must be "need-oriented" planners. They must be willing to adapt. They must seek to be creative. Their total energies must not be spent on perpetuating the past. They must exploit change.

For leaders of growing churches change is not a threat but a life-style. Testing the functional validity of a plan, program, activity, or philosophy is commonplace to them. (See the functional validity test in the process manual.) These learn to present change with skill, enthusiasm, and Christian dignity. This is not a Madison Avenue technique. It is a basic principle to the very life and growth of the church.

James Glasse has given some helpful guidelines on how to calculate the risks of change.

> If I say/do what? _____
> I will run a _____ % risk of losing _____ members (name them) and $_____ money and a _____ % risk of losing my job.

The church leader must be able to calculate the risk if he is to run the risk responsibly. This requires the construction of an "Equation" by which the risk can be calculated. With practice any pastor can learn to do it.

1. How many members he can afford to lose, and still maintain a viable congregation.

2. How much money he can afford to lose from the church budget.

3. How much personal income he can afford to lose and still meet his financial obligations.

4. How much public acceptance, respect and affection he is prepared to sacrifice for his convictions.

5. How much public censure he and his family can tolerate.

6. How much physical danger he is prepared to suffer.[6]

Expansion, extension, and bridging growth introduce challenges to the status quo of the church that makes evaluating and changing everyday experiences.

The principle of new units is a basic principle of church growth.

New people are new units.

A new person, reached by the church, provides a new arena in which to work. This is primarily true with regards to those reached through transfer of membership and conversion. New people who come to the church through transfer growth can create many contexts for growth:

—A relocated church member can bring a new need to his or her new church.

—A relocated church member can bring an entire family into the church by transfer of membership.

—A relocated church member can bring a new set of community relationships.

—A relocated church member can bring a new leader to the church.

This same growth can and does result when a new convert is reached by the church. Often the zeal and enthusiasm of this person creates a chain of events that will stimulate growth.

—Newly converted people usually come from groups of people who are not being touched by the ministry of the church. Therefore, their friendships open new avenues for growth.

—Newly converted people have the thrill of the newness of the new life in Christ.

—Newly converted people express strong loyalty to the church through attendance and participation.

—Newly converted people have a contagious enthusiasm that more settled members do not have.

—Newly converted people have a fresh and dynamic testimony of the activity of God in their lives. They appear to look for God's activity in their lives.

—Newly converted people have tremendous capacities for personal growth.

New people reach their relatives and friends and encourage the existing church family to reach out with new vigor. Nothing can stimulate church growth more rapidly than new people being reached.

New organizational units are part of the new unit principle of church growth.

God has fashioned a strategy for growth. For want of better terms we must define it by saying, "He multiplies by dividing." Church organizations expand by dividing large units into smaller units. They also expand by creating new units where none previously existed. This type of expansion creates new growth contexts.

Organizational process tends to develop along the following lines:
* A Creative Phase
* A Management Phase
* A Legalistic Phase
* A Destructive Phase

The most important process phase is the Creative Phase. This keeps the organization and its leaders alive to new possibilities. This tends to keep the church aware of its needs to survive and grow.

The Management Phase tends to find its functional focus in keeping all things orderly and efficient.

Following the Management Phase is usually the drawing up of strict rules or guidelines that become of major importance. The enforcement of or adherence to these rules and guidelines become ends in themselves.

The painful process of destruction is the next step. Something has developed an adversary climate and creativity is usually born out of a painful decision brought about by the destructive phase.

An organization can maintain a constantly creative focus if new unit development is considered top priority.

Growing churches seek ways to involve people in service. Growing churches have departments, classes, and groups that accomplish more in small group situations than in larger corporate settings. In growing churches specific groups are organized to meet specific needs. These may be called task forces.

Increasing delegation of responsibilities will usually result in new organizational units. As new needs arise, new organizational units emerge to meet those needs.

It is a fact of life in the growing church that present organizational structures cannot meet all future needs. So, the new unit is a natural part of organizational growth.

New extension and bridging units are part of the new unit principle of church growth.

Growing churches are aware of opportunities to extend a witness beyond their own facility and location. They are conscious of needs to involve money and personnel beyond the week-by-week activities of their own church.

Growing churches look for ways to meet needs that cannot be met through the Sunday program.

New Bible study groups, preaching points, potential chapel or church locations are concerns of a growing church.

The churches that will grow significantly in the future will be aware of the need for bridging across cultural, racial, economic, and social barriers with new units specifically designed to meet needs in those areas.

Conclusion

There is no exhaustive nor ultimate study of all the church growth principles that exist and how they produce growth. All that can be said is, when these principles or some principles like them are applied to a church, growth takes place.

You may discover new ones. Someone like you discovered these. God wants churches to grow through the multiplication of the number of its members. He likewise desires growth among its members as they link their lives to him, his Word and the members of his church.

As Wyn Arn has said in his workshops, "Let's Grow!"

4
How to Get Out of a Holding Pattern

American Flight 269 was right on schedule. It departed New York—LaGuardia—on time, served a wonderful meal as it flew west across the mountains and arrived over Chicago's O'Hare in time to be at the gate at 7:36 P.M. But the front from a low pressure system arrived twenty minutes earlier. Due to severe snow conditions, mighty O'Hare was socked in, closed to all traffic. Flight 269 went into a holding pattern. For two hours it flew in a long ellipse out over Lake Michigan. Eventually the plane had to land in St. Louis.

A church as well as an airliner can be halted on the way to its goals. That which happens every day to travelers and sometimes lasts several hours, happens every week to churches and sometimes lasts for decades. A church may travel in circles, maintaining its altitude for a time. But, finally, it too will run out of gas. Usually its final destination is nowhere near its original objective.

The analogy between airliner and church will soon break down. But we may well ask, "Is it possible for a church to get out of a holding pattern and to get on to its goals, or even to goals greater than it ever had?" Indeed, some churches find themselves in a holding pattern and never have had identifiable goals.

The answer, we insist, is yes. Here are eight steps any church can take to get off its own private, aerial merry-go-round and begin to go somewhere besides *in decline*.

I

Diagnose the growth record of your church.

First, let us *insist* that you take these words seriously. A "diagnosis," according to Webster, is a "careful investigation of the facts to determine the nature of a thing." To diagnose is to discover by meticulous examination and careful observation the real character of a thing. To diagnose the growth record of a church is to take a hard look at how a church is growing—not just in general, but in all its various and particular segments.

To "insist" is necessary because of what Donald A. McGavran has called, a "universal fog" shrouding church growth.[1] This fog keeps us from seeing how well or how poorly we are actually doing in the central task of making disciples and adding them to the church.

What gives rise to the fog? One of several factors can hinder us from perceptive clarity in reference to growth.

1. Advance in the level of giving year by year in your church may prove deceptive. A period of inflation, a time of national or regional economic growth, or the upward movement of people to middle class may give the illusion of church growth.

2. Evangelistic methods that have become a tradition in the annual church calendar may only appear to be growth-producing.

3. Progress in improving the cultural standards of the educational or music program of the church may be conceived as growth.

4. Incessant church sponsored activities within a congregation, no matter how good they may be, can create a smoke screen to keep people from thinking about growth or nongrowth.

5. Preoccupation with creating *koinonia* in the congregation can obscure the need and dull the passion for adding newly regenerate men and women to the church. New Testament *koinonia* was always contagious. *Koinonia* that is focused only inward has not captured the genius of the first-century variety.

6. Church administration that majors on efficiency without consideration of effectiveness may disparage church growth and actually keep the church from perceiving the nature of its evangelistic penetration, or lack of penetration, of the unchurched community.

7. Success in biological and transfer growth may delude the casual observer and feed the emotional needs of the membership.

8. Interest in and support of overseas missionary projects may keep churches from an honest look at their record in their own community.

9. The real growth situation can be shrouded in fog because of a disinterest in statistics. This is often motivated by a genuine desire to care more for individuals than "nickels and noses."

Facts are absolutely essential to an informed strategy for breaking out of a holding pattern. The diagnosis will require exact and painstaking research. This is the only way facts are secured.

What kind of facts? At least these seven questions are of crucial importance and must be answered with precision if an accurate diagnosis is to be made:

Has the church been growing?

What has been the rate of growth?

How has the church been adding members?

How has our church been losing members?

Where have our new church members come from?

What kind of leadership do we have?

How do we spend our time?

The following chapter will discuss these questions in detail.

Proper records are so important! Most churches keep very inadequate records for assessing actual church growth. Yet facts are essential to dispelling the haze and mist that keep us from seeing the growth history of a congregation. For this reason, keeping better records today will pay handsome dividends in the future.

Improved record keeping should begin at the moment a new member is received in the church. Using an Addition Analysis Form ten minutes with each new member, as he is added to the church, will provide the facts you will need next year, or five years from now, when you do another diagnosis of the growth of your church.[2] The form, filled out in detail, will provide excellent leads for potential growth right now.

II

Analyze these growth facts.

Why is as significant as *what* in church growth. To have discovered what has actually happened is essential but not sufficient. The facts and figures tallied must be examined critically and minutely. That is just what it means to do an analysis.

At least two things are necessary to arrive at a helpful evaluation of the facts that have been discovered. First, the facts have to be broken down into segments. Understanding of the whole diagnosis is achieved by looking carefully at the various parts. Secondly, we need to learn the fine art of *exact attribution.* Men habitually assign cause to facts as they discover them, usually with very little precision. Analysis demands that we abandon this penchant for instant judgment. To "attribute" means "to ascribe as resulting from, owing to or caused by." We must learn *exact attribution.* What did this or that fact result from? Three basic questions must be asked over and over again: Why? When? How? Why did your church grow between 1971 and 1974? Why did it decline after 1974?

When did the rate of growth begin to taper off? How soon did that effect the numerical growth? Why did the church have an upsurge of conversion growth in 1971? What contributed to the large number of transfers from the church in 1974? Why have most of our new members come from new subdivisions? Why have so few come from the community where the church building is located? All these are questions that enable us to ascribe cause exactly. You will discover many more as you look at the figures carefully.

You will find that the answers to six more questions will greatly assist your analysis. Have this information before you as you begin the process.

1. What men have served as pastors of this church and what was the month and year each man began and ended his ministry?

2. What other staff members have been added and when did their ministries begin and end?

3. When were new buildings built or acquired and occupied?

4. Has the church had a significant division and when did the rupture take place?

5. What daughter churches has the church begun and during what periods were the new congregations being nurtured?

6. When did these new congregations become autonomous bodies and how many were transferred from the membership of the mother church? [3]

III

Know the character and life-style of your church.

To break out of a holding pattern, nothing will substitute for a thorough self-knowledge. This is a third essential step. Here are four suggestions that will contribute to this self-understanding.

First, *identify your church type.* Ezra Earl Jones has isolated six types of churches on the American scene among which almost any congregation can find itself.[4]

1. Old First Church Downtown is found in the central business district of the city and may draw members from all the residential areas of a city.

2. Neighborhood Church is located in a residential community of a city or suburb and draws its members primarily from that area.

3. Metropolitan-Regional Church is situated strategically at the growing edge of a metropolitan area and is growing rapidly usually among the middle class. It may draw its members from all parts of the metropolitan community but will usually have most from the area of town where it is located.

4. Special Purpose Church structures its life around particular issues, doctrines, life-styles, or cultural characteristics. It attracts people who want its unique kind of ministry. They will often travel a great distance to attend.

5. Small Town Church is much like the downtown church except that the community is much smaller. Because the small town is often itself one neighborhood, it has some of the characteristics of the neighborhood church as well.

6. Open Country Church is in the open country, serving a sparsely settled area but may minister also to people who have moved to a nearby town or city and prefer to return to worship at the "old home church."

Most churches will fall into one of these types. If your church does not fit exactly in one of these descriptions it is probably in transition between two of them.

It will be very helpful for you to identify the church type that best describes your church situation. That in itself may help you understand some of the reasons your church is growing or declining. A neighborhood church in a saturated, static community may find itself static. Many churches are special interest churches and are not even aware of it. If you only address your ministry to a scattered cultural or socioeconomic group, the growth of your church can be restricted by that limited clientele.

Second, *understand the ministry life-style of your congregation.* How do you approach people with the gospel of Jesus Christ? What is your philosophy of ministry?

Indeed, the ministry life-style, especially in smaller, younger churches, is likely to vary according to the style of pastoral leadership. Do not, however, make the mistake of automatically identifying the pastor's philosophy of ministry with that of the church. Unless the pastor has served for a considerable period of time, the two may be worlds apart. The difference will quickly surface if the congregation begins to grow. Conflict is an inevitable result.

How important is it to understand the ministry life-style of your church? Extremely. If the philosophy of ministry is essentially self-destructive, that is, turned in toward maintenance of the existing situation and not turned out toward the unchurched, then it will need to be changed. Without understanding the reigning philosophy it will be difficult to estimate what needs to be done and how to go about it.

Several questions may be asked that will aid in developing understanding. Is your church program conventional or innovative? Do you follow a denominational line or sometimes create your own programs? Do you

71

have open invitations for public decisions? Are there regular weeks of evangelistic services? Is your educational program aimed at outreach or edification?

Third, *acknowledge the basic homogeneous unit of your church.* Much more will be said about this concept later. However, recognition of its importance is helpful in getting out of a holding pattern. A homogeneous unit (HU) is simply a section of society in which all the members have some characteristic in common.[5] Almost without exception, churches basically belong to one HU. A few members may be part of another HU, but the larger body of disciples in a given congregation inevitably belong to one major unit of society.

This is important because churches grow more quickly among people from their predominant HU. People in the church's HU are near neighbors and no barriers of consequence have to be crossed to witness and evangelize these people.

However, this growth principle can actually hinder growth if the HU is small and if a church steadfastly refuses to welcome into its fellowship those from other HU's that are responsive to the gospel.

When a family is won to Christ and church membership from another HU, this should be recognized immediately and determined efforts be made to win additional new families from that same unit so the E-1 evangelism can go on among that new group.

Finally, *recognize the spiritual gifts present in your congregation.* The spontaneous expansion of the church, or a local congregation, is related directly to the proper function of the various parts of the body. "We are to grow up in every way into him who is the head, into Christ, from whom the whole body, . . . when each part is working properly, makes bodily growth and upbuilds itself in love" (Eph. 4:15–16, RSV). To be aware of the gifts present in a given congregation is of crucial importance. Leaders of churches that have grown significantly have very often been persons who recognized gifts in others and have been able to challenge them to exercise those gifts.

The major biblical material on gifts is found in Romans 12, 1 Corinthians 12, and Ephesians 4. The lists overlap, but each one adds to our knowledge. Combined together the list looks something like this:

Apostleship	Discernment
Prophecy	Tongues
Evangelism	Interpretation of tongues
Pastoral	Ministry helps

Teaching	Administration
Wisdom	Exhortation
Knowledge	Liberality
Faith	Mercy
Healing	Service
Miracles	

There is no reason to believe that this list is exhaustive. The gifts of the Holy Spirit are diverse (Rom. 12:6) and varied (1 Cor. 12:4). They are for the common good (1 Cor. 12:7). The list of gifts could go on and on.

We do know that every Christian is gifted (1 Cor. 12:7). Because of those gifts, every Christian has a ministry to perform and the grace to perform that ministry successfully (Rom. 12:6).

The presence of gifts in a church determines the kinds of ministries that can be undertaken. The discovery of gifts in a congregation and willingness to exercise those gifts are big steps out of a holding pattern.

IV

Know your community.

To gain a thorough knowledge of the community in which a church is located and to which it plans to minister is the next step necessary for breaking out of a holding pattern. A church needs to become familiar with its community from at least three perspectives.

First, develop a profile of the *social characteristics* of your community. Government and community agencies can provide inestimable help at this point. You will find the planning commission of your city delighted when they learn that your church is really interested in the social make-up of your area. They will gladly share information they have with you.

However, the ultimate source of such information is the most recent United States census. Become familiar with its documents and learn to use them. You will be able to find in it the basic information needed for each town and city above 2,500 in population and, if you live in a large city, and need to focus on a more restricted area, on each census tract.

Your community is a mosaic of many varied parts. Information obtainable from the census and useful for a good understanding of your area will include:

1. Population figures
2. Housing characteristics
3. Age characteristics

4. Racial composition
5. Ethnic composition
6. Family size and structure
7. Family income levels
8. Employment characteristics
9. Nativity and mobility information
10. Educational attainment levels [6]

A warning is needed here. *Do not make the mistake of permitting this information to dictate the ministries of your church.* This information is primarily valuable in telling you what kind of community you live in. It helps you identify the socioeconomic, cultural, and racial segments of your area. To determine ministries, you must know your community in another way.

The second perspective for knowing your community is *felt need*. Thorough familiarity with the social characteristics of your area is, by itself, an inadequate platform from which to overcome arrested growth. It is inadequate for formulating any ministry in the name of Jesus Christ. At this point, most community surveys fail the church.

A church in a holding pattern is a church in the throes of an effectiveness crisis. For various, perhaps complex, reasons, energy is not being expended for growth or the energy that is being exerted is nonproductive. The church may be organized and even function very efficiently. The pastor may be an able administrator. Yet the congregation is ineffective in growth and reproduction. Peter F. Drucker has helpfully distinguished between effectiveness and efficiency. "Effectiveness is the foundation of success—efficiency is a minimum condition for survival . . . Efficiency is concerned with doing things right. Effectiveness is doing the right things." [7]

One of the primary causes of an effectiveness crisis in churches is one-way communication. The message is going out, but few are listening. At least, few are responding positively. Few are being persuaded to believe in Christ and become members of his church.

One-way communication takes place, marketing specialists have demonstrated, when the focus is on the *product*, or the *message*, without reference to the *audience*. Paul had learned this truth long before marketing professionals came on the scene. This is evident from his words in 1 Corinthians 9:22, "Whatever a person is like, I try to find common ground with him so that he will let me tell him about Christ and let Christ save him" (TLB).

People do see and hear what they want to see and hear. Every person

74

has what has been called a "God-given filter" through which he processes all the messages that come through the senses. Only when the message and/or ministry is addressed to *felt need* in an individual is that filter open so the message can get through.[8] Coming to know the felt need of the community makes it possible to overcome one-way communication. Message and ministry can be addressed to people where their filters are open. People, then, can, and do, respond. Discovering felt need makes it possible for us to focus on our *audience* as well as our *message*.

Success in any endeavor, according to Robert H. Schuller's maxim, is finding a need and filling it. That church that discovers where people are hurting and meets that need in the name of and with the message of Jesus Christ deserves to succeed. The big question is not, How can we get these people to accept the message? That is the wrong question! The big question is, Where are these people conscious of pain and how is Jesus Christ good news to that situation? What can we do to heal the open wounds and throbbing aches of the people in our community? Our focus must be on needs people feel, not those we perceive. How can we serve people in Christ's name in ways they will recognize our service?

How do you discover felt need in your community? At least two possibilities are available. The first is to develop an effective questionnaire that will reveal areas of responsiveness and isolate the problem areas in the community where people are looking for a solution. Some method will need to be devised to get a response from an adequate sampling of the community. From the information provided a church can develop its audience-centered strategy.[9]

The second method is not as sophisticated but can be as effective in the hands of perceptive persons.[10] Take two to four weeks and go house-to-house. Major on those who do not belong to anyone's church. Ask questions, listen, and take notes. Find out where these people hurt and hunger. Let them tell you about their anxieties, fear, and aspirations. Visit door-to-door six hours a day, listen carefully, and in three weeks you will begin to have a composite picture of where people feel need. You can then use that information to adopt a strategy of ministry and growth.

The third perspective from which you need to know your community is in reference to *those within it who are unchurched*. Unchurched people, not those of your own denomination who may be transferred into your area, are the key that will enable your church to break out of its holding pattern. Underline this last sentence. It is an axiom. You don't need an influx of Baptists or Methodists or Evangelicals. You need to be successful in introducing Jesus Christ to those who do not know him. Therefore, it is most important to know who these people are and what barriers exist between them and your church. Develop a diagram that will tell you just how "far" these people are from your congregation. By "far" we mean not merely a geographical distance, but cultural and social distance as well.

How do you go about this? Take the following five steps.

1. Estimate the unchurched population in your community or city. Suppose you live in a city of 100,000. You can discover what percentage of that population are actually members of a Christian body. For the United States in 1976 that percentage was 59.2. Using that figure you can determine that 40,800 in a city of 100,000 do not belong to any Christian group. Realistically, at least one out of four in most American churches shows no evidence of genuine Christian commitment. You may wish to add one fourth of the churched population to the total picture. In a city of 100,000 that would mean about 66,600 people with no vital allegiance to Jesus Christ.

If you wish to be more exact and to have an even more astonishing figure, do a church profile of your town.[11] Contact every church, find the membership of each, and then discover how many attend on an average Sunday. Compare this figure to the population. You will find that less than 20 percent are usually in worship on a given Sunday, unless your community is extraordinary. There are millions of people who need Christ in America. Many of them are in your town.

2. Discover how many unchurched people are too far away from you geographically for you to effectively win them to Christ. On a map, draw three concentric circles around the building where your church meets. Give one the radius of five miles, another ten miles, and the third fifteen miles. Using census tracts, or some other method, find out how many people are in each one of those circles. Estimate the number who are unchurched exactly as in step one.

Those who live over twenty minutes (between ten and fifteen miles) from your church building are usually at too great a geographical distance for your church to witness to them effectively. Good Christians may travel over twenty minutes to worship and serve in your church but few non-Christians will do it. Focus on the unchurched in that ten-mile radius.

3. Identify those who are a significant ethnic distance from your congregation. Suppose that in the ten-mile radius of your church building there are 4,000 unchurched people who speak Spanish in their homes while your congregation has English as its heart language. Endeavor to win all the Spanish-speaking people you can to Christ and responsible membership in your church. Nevertheless, recognize that such efforts

will involve E-2 evangelism and will require something besides near neighbor witnessing. Scattered families may be evangelized by your congregation and added to your church. But your congregation may need to become involved in bridging growth if it wants to effectively address the gospel to that entire language-culture community.

4. Be candid in counting those unchurched people in a ten-mile radius of your church who may be so socially or economically distanced from you that they will not comfortably become Christians within your congregation.

This must not be construed as an effort to create class churches. Your church should attempt to win everyone to Christ and membership in that ten-mile radius. Your church may be open to gladly receive members from every culture and social strata. What your church is willing to do on this issue is not the point. What are the felt needs of this group of unchurched people? Men do not like to cross cultural barriers to become Christians, nor should they be forced to do so. To win them to Christ and membership in your church may require a situation in which they can become Christians among their peers.

Use the profile of social characteristics to compile these figures. If your church is composed mainly of factory workers, you should isolate that subdivision of upper-bracket homes on five acre lots as a community that may involve special efforts at evangelism.

Use the profile of social characteristics to compile these figures. If your church is composed mainly of factory workers, you should isolate that subdivision of upper-bracket homes on five acre lots as a community that may involve special efforts at evangelism.

5. Now, using the figure that you have compiled, count up those unchurched people in your community who are not culturally, socially, or geographically distant from your congregation. They should have first priority in your advance out of a holding pattern.

V

Dream a realistic but challenging dream.

The first four steps have accumulated facts. You uncovered the growth record of your church. You have some estimate of its character and personality. You have gained a new perception of your community. Now take a look into the future.

From the planning agency of your city, county, or state discover what the projections are for population growth or decline in your community for the next five, ten, and even twenty years. With these figures you can estimate what the unchurched population will be. You will probably be able also to have some estimate of the social make-up of the immediate community of your church building by those dates.

This information and what you have previously discovered about your church and community is the platform from which dreams can be dreamed and vision can be acquired. Do not underestimate the power and importance of a dream. *It will be impossible for your church to get out of its holding pattern without a dream.* Someone must have a vision of the good, the wonderful, and the possible that is in the future of your church.

What is a dream or a vision? It is a mental picture of a future reality. In the context of Christian discipleship and church growth, our frame of reference, we are interested only in Spirit-inspired dreams and God-given visions. Therefore, if the leadership of your church has no dream for your church, begin to ask God immediately to share his purpose for your church with them. From this perspective a vision becomes a kind of promise of what is to be. It is an image of the divine intention.

A dream may be personal at the beginning, that is, it may be a vision given to one person, but it must become corporate. It will have to be communicated to, shared with, and eventually owned by others.

Furthermore, a dream given by God's Spirit to a church or a church leader is usually conditional. Take David and the perpetuity of his earthly throne as an example. One of the psalms records it:

> The Lord has sworn to David,
> A truth from which He will not turn back;
> "Of the fruit of your body I will set up your throne.
> If your sons will keep my covenant,
> And My testimony which I will teach them,
> There sons shall also sit upon your throne forever" (Ps. 132:11–12, NASB).

That was a magnificent vision and a bold promise. It was given to an individual, and it became corporate, held by the entire nation. But it was conditional. Eventually, some of the descendents rejected the terms of the vision.

Most of the visions you receive for the future of your church will be conditioned on your faithfulness to God now and in the years ahead. They will also have to be communicated to the corporate body of the congregation.

How does this take place?

Begin with your leadership. We suggest that you involve them in a retreat situation for sixteen or twenty-four hours so that they can give undivided attention to the full diagnosis of the present situation and a prognosis about the future.[12] Some leaders, of course, will be involved in gathering the data, but as many of the decision-makers as possible need to be involved in a careful look at the results of the research.

As dramatically and graphically as possible let them see, hear, and feel (also, taste and smell, if possible):

Where you, as the church, have been.

How you are doing.

What you are.

What you have.

Where you are right now.

Take plenty of time. Dream together about where and what the church could be in twenty years. Draw a big picture that looks out into the future. What would need to be achieved in ten years? Then, focus in on five years. Under the blessing of God, following dynamic leadership, and with determined efforts, what could you achieve that would give glory to God, meet felt need, and cause the body of Christ to grow in the next five years?

Turn loose the God-given creative imagination of the leaders of your church. What would they dream for their church if money were no object of consideration and you know that you could not fail? Write it all down. Dream big dreams. You can never achieve more than someone dares to dream.

Now, two cautions. Remember the context of your dreaming. The entire atmosphere should be one of much praying. Ask for *divine* guidance for the *divine* intention for your church. The Bible is full of promises from God that he will guide those who will commit themselves to follow him. The first and primary consideration is, What will please God?

Secondly, your dream must be realistic. Don't plan for a church with an average attendance of 5,000 in a county of 4,500. Don't build a building for 5,000 middle-class whites in a community that will be black or Chicano in seven years. Rather dream for a ministry in that kind of community. One of the reasons for research is to be able to dream realistic, but challenging, dreams.

VI

Turn your dreams into goals that will stretch your faith.

79

Explaining this step requires an answer to three questions. What is a goal? How do dreams become goals? Why stretch faith?

A goal is a response to a perceived need. It, too, is an image or picture of what the future might be or how it might be shaped. But a goal involves more than either of these two definitions suggests. It is a future event that can be accomplished and towards which you can make measurable progress. It may grow out of a general purpose or objective, it may reflect or express a God-given dream, but it must be achievable and is, therefore, measurable. You can always determine whether or not a goal has been reached and just how much progress, if any, has been made toward its completion.

To be actually measurable, a goal must also be dated. It has a target completion time. That this is essential will become evident if the achievement of a goal is assigned to an individual or group, or if it is a part of a hierarchy of goals that move the church toward a larger goal or general objective. With no completion date there can be no accountability or realistic measurement of progress. With no target completion time, it is impossible to say for sure that you have failed or to press on to completion.

"To make Chicago Christian" may be a far-reaching, laudable objective. But it cannot be measured. "To personally share the claims of Christ with the heads of 14,000 unchurched families in the Lake View Community of Chicago by September 1, 1980" is a goal. It is achievable, measurable, and dated. It is a response to perceived need. Fourteen thousand families who have had a warm personal contact with someone from a church and have heard the good news of Jesus Christ in terms they can understand is a desirable, new shape for the future in Lake View or any other community.

A dream becomes a goal when it is made public. To announce your dream involves commitment. Consequently, this step is much easier said than done. No goal should ever be announced to a church that doesn't have the commitment of those who make the pronouncement. To make a goal believable, to make it saleable, to move it along toward ownership by the entire group, demands undiluted dedication to it. The men who signed the Declaration of Independence were announcing their dream. A new, independent nation was their goal. To that they pledged their lives, property, and fortunes. It cost some of those men exactly what they pledged, but the goal became believable with that level of commitment.

Getting a church out of a holding pattern involves this kind of commitment as well. If the decision-makers of the church are actually led to dream formulation, through the study of the church and community research, and then will announce those dreams, backing them up with total dedication to them, the congregation as a whole is sure to own the goals as well.

Many Christians are afraid to set goals. Setting definite, measurable goals with a time for completing them also creates the risk of failure. The fear of failure is a fantastic deterrent to faith as well as activity. It is a tyrant in the lives of many Christians that not only intimidates them, but keeps them from making glad and positive responses. The fear of failure holds men in bondage.

This fear may express itself in several ways. Some leaders will absolutely refuse to set goals. Others will respond by setting goals so small that their achievement is sure. No risk is involved. Still others will want goals so large they are unachievable. This eliminates risk as surely as low goals. An easy excuse is always available. The goals were too large in the beginning.

To offset these expressions of the fear of failure, goal-setting needs to become an act of faith. The faith of most Christians is so meager, especially in churches caught in a holding pattern, that it needs to be stretched.

Goal-setting in a church should never be arbitrary but always turned Godward. Ask the group of decision-makers to spend considerable time in personal and small group praying. Let them ask for direct and definite leadership from God. Ask God to guide by the *concensus of his children* or by a sure *promise from his word.* The presence and leadership of the Holy Spirit creating unity of purpose in a group so that there is oneness of mind about a goal stretches and strengthens faith. The conviction that some promise from the word of God has direct application to the present situation does the same.

While you should avoid the temptation to set goals so large that there is no expectation of achievement, do adopt goals that are beyond the attainment of dedicated human effort. The goals should be large enough that when they are achieved there will be recognition that God has been at work among and through his people. The recognition of God's hand in the achievement of otherwise impossible goals stretches and establishes faith.

VII

Mobilize your membership for growth.

Kenneth Strachan, an important missionary leader during this century, observed from his study of the growth of Communism, Jehovah's Witnesses, and Pentecostal churches in South America that the *growth of any movement is in direct proportion to the ability of that movement to mobilize its total membership in the constant propagation of its beliefs.*[13]

There is considerable evidence that the most famous missionary expression of that principle, evangelism in depth, did not prove as productive in terms of the growth of churches, as it was hoped.[14] Nevertheless, the axiom remains essentially true.

The axiom does not mean that every member must be engaged in evangelistic visitation. Only about 10 percent of a given congregation are really gifted to be harvesters.[15] It does mean that every Christian should be a witness to the power of Jesus in his life today and be able to share that life through some God-given ministry with others.

How do you mobilize your membership for growth? Neil Braun, in a pivotal book on the place of laypersons in church growth, made five suggestions that will prove helpful here.[16]

1. Preserve original zeal by involving new Christians at once in personal witness and evangelism among their peers, friends, and kinfolk.

2. Nurture the membership in the necessary skills of the Christian life: how to pray, how to read and apply the Bible to life, how to live a cleansed life, and how to be lead by the Holy Spirit.

3. Get broad participation of as many members as possible in the spiritual ministry of the church. Don't just involve the membership in the maintenance jobs of the congregation, those ministries, some of them essential, to the church as it is. Focus participation on those ministries that are turned out toward the world.

4. Learn the technique of withdrawal. The professional staff should give lay leadership significant responsibilities and let them function in performance of them without interference.

5. Train, motivate, and create an atmosphere in the membership for evangelism. Significant growth never takes place in a congregation or a group of congregations until those unordained, unsalaried leaders whom God has gifted as harvesters are equipped to exercise their gift.

VIII

Use methods being made effective by the blessing of God.

Holding on to evangelistic methods and church organizations that are no longer effective is one factor that contributes to a holding pattern. The final step essential to breaking the bondage of no growth is to find and use methods that are marked by the Spirit of God with growth effectiveness at the present time.

It is easy for methods, organizations and institutional procedures to take on the aura of sanctity. A church can have Bible study at 9:30 A.M. and worship at 10:45 A.M. on Sunday morning for so long that it assumes this has always been the case and, in fact, was the first century pattern. The Wednesday night prayer meeting has become an institution among evangelicals during the last 125 years. It is sometimes considered so sacred that it cannot be abandoned, for one week, for a prayer program that would involve ten times as many people praying. An institution can become an end in itself.

The key to breaking a holding pattern is to use methods *God is blessing*. Methods are never eternal. That which was effective in the past may not be effective now or in the future. During the Great Awakening, the monthly lecture was the instrument used over and over again to begin revival and growth. Very few growing or nongrowing churches use that method today.

No method is universal. Not all methods work in all places with equal effectiveness. Culture and life-style are human factors to be considered. Many churches that are growing significantly have week-long evangelistic meetings with regularity. Others growing just as significantly never use that method. A church that wishes to move on toward growth goals needs to discover those methods being blessed by God in their area. Then, they need to assess that method in light of their own life-style and the unchurched community to which they minister. Finally, and most importantly, they need to seek, through deliberate, concerted prayer, the will of God for their church in reference to the methods that seem to be presently most effective. Just because a bus ministry is a major tool in one congregation does not necessarily mean it is the method God intends for your congregation. Only by committing itself to the lordship and leadership of Christ can the church find the methods God intends to bless in its ministry.

One secret of spontaneous growth is to find out what God is doing in the world and then join him in his work. God only blesses with fantastic effectiveness what he initiates himself. These three steps can help us discover what he is doing.

1. Find out what he is blessing.
2. Evaluate that method in the light of your church and the unchurched community.

3. Seek the guidance of the Holy Spirit in adapting methods to your church.

Recapitulation

How can a church get out of a holding pattern? We have described eight steps that we believe will enable churches to break the pattern of arrested growth or decline. As you have read them you are aware that they combine an objective, scientific evaluation of church and community with a subjective, distinctively spiritual, sensitivity to the will and way of the risen Christ. Let us stress that you take each step very seriously. Take no shortcuts! Do not neglect the factual research. Do not compromise in the obedience of faith.

Just for review, here are the eight steps again.

1. Diagnose the growth record of your church.
2. Analyze these growth facts.
3. Know the character and life-style of your church.
4. Know your community.
5. Dream a realistic but challenging dream.
6. Turn your dreams into goals that will stretch your faith.
7. Mobilize your membership for growth.
8. Use methods being made effective by the blessing of God.

5
How to Diagnose the Growth Health of Your Church

In medical terms a diagnosis is the determination of a disease by a comprehensive examination of the patient. Accurate diagnosis is the foundation of modern medicine. Proper treatment is only possible when the cause of an illness is known.

Diagnosis begins by making an exhaustive study of the patient's heredity, health history, and habits. This investigation is followed by a thorough physical examination of the patient and by having him undergo a battery of tests. These tests may include checking the skin for immune or nonimmune reactions. Physical examinations may be supplemented by X rays and such special instruments as the stethoscope, bronchoscope, electrocardiograph, or devices for testing basal metabolism. Tissue specimens may be examined microscopically and, along with specimens of blood and excreta, may be cultured to discover the presence of microorganisms. From this assembled data and knowledge of the characteristic symptoms of diseases, a skilled diagnostician is usually able to determine the disease present in the patient.[1]

Comparable procedure is necessary to determine the growth health of a church. There are at least seven tests that need to be made on your church that will enable you to determine the likelihood of a growth-disease and to pinpoint areas where there is growth-health. Problem areas must be identified before growth solutions can be discovered.

This approach, of course, makes nonsensical the objection that concern with statistics is unimportant, unnecessary, or carnal. Statistics are never an end in themselves. They are essential to the discovery of ill health.

> To be sure, no one was ever saved by statistics; but then, no one was ever cured by the thermometer to which the physician pays such close attention. X-ray pictures never knit a single broken bone, yet they are of considerable value to physicians in telling them how to put the two ends of a fractured bone together. Similarly, the facts of

growth will not in themselves lead anyone to Christ. But they can be of marked value to any Church which desires to know where, when and how to carry on its work so that maximum increase of soundly Christian churches will result.[2]

I

The Numbers Test

The first test answers the question: Has your church been growing or has it been in decline? This question must be answered before diagnosis or further testing can continue. Very little research and only the simplest arithmetic are required to supply an answer.

1. Begin by collecting the membership and attendance totals of your church. Gather the information for the last ten years at least. You may want to study the entire history of your congregation. There are several types of information that can be helpful. The level of sophistication adopted by your research will be determined by your time, interest, and the kind of records you have. If time and statistical data are sufficient, we suggest that you gather the following totals:

1. Total membership (We refer to communicant membership, of course.)
2. Resident membership
3. Nonresident membership
4. Average Sunday morning worship attendance
5. Sunday School enrollment
6. Average Sunday School attendance.[3]

Most of this information is easily discovered. It becomes the data base for several of the remaining tests. It can be found in the annual reports your church makes to a local association, synod, or conference of churches. Usually this information is published in booklet form and is easily accessible.

It may be that you will prefer to develop a composite membership figure by averaging items 2, 4, and 6 above. A composite figure probably does provide a more realistic assessment of what is really happening in a church. However, few churches have readily available all three factors necessary for composite totals. We believe an adequate and reliable picture of the growth health of your church can be developed by the use of resident membership totals.

Get these numbers if at all possible. Most churches in America have a significant number of nonresident members. These "members," if they are such, are not available for any of the church's ministries. When "resident members" become "nonresident members," that church has actually lost those members. So, it is important, if you are to get a true picture of your church, to deal with *resident membership facts.*

If the only information you have is in total membership, then proceed with that, but be aware that some adjustment may have to be made to have a realistic picture. (See Figure 1 for a sample how this collected information will look.) It will be helpful to collect all of this information if it is available. Then you can make an informed decision about which totals provide the most accurate data for the remainder of the tests.

Figure 1

Years	This Year	Last Year	-2	-3	-4	-5	-6	-7	-8	-9	-10
Total Membership	290	252	240	222	325	237	230	216	215	201	172
Resident Membership	240	210	200	180	260	220	190	160	170	160	140

2. Plot the growth on a simple graph. Collected figures say very little to the average observer. The facts must be *graphically* displayed.

The process is simple. On a piece of graph paper draw a vertical and horizontal scale (these are really the two positive poles of an axis). Plot your membership along the vertical line, making sure that each section represents an equal number of the total. The scale can be adjusted, depending on the size of your church. (See Figure 2.) Along the horizontal line indicate the years in question.

Now, using your data, pinpoint the membership figure for each year and connect each one of the dots with a bold line. Before you is an accurate drawing, a picture, of the growth of your church over the period in question.

3. Analyze your growth or decline. Using the full information you have previously collected about your church, explain any sudden or persistent growth or loss pattern for one or several years. What happened in the church or community to assist in the growth of your congregation? What contributed to decline? Take each distinct pattern and engage in *exact attribution.* Use the information you have gathered about dates when pastors have come or gone, when new buildings have been occupied, and when divisions have occurred. You know what took place. Now attempt to ascribe cause. But remember, it may be none of these!

Figure 2

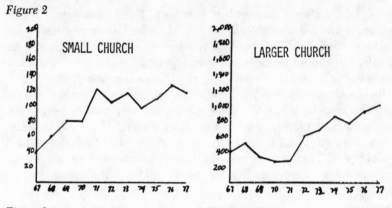

Figure 3

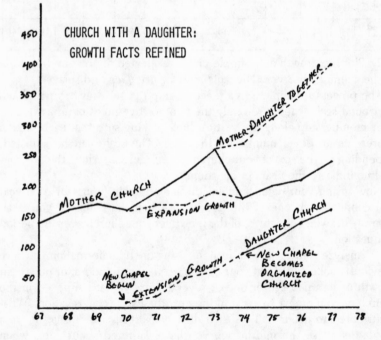

Do not be surprised if decline or no growth for a year or two follows the construction and occupation of a new building. This is most often what really happens after a building is completed.

4. Church membership totals provide essential and helpful information, but they can be misleading. Very often your effort to analyze these facts will require that the figures be refined. You may discover that a sudden drop in membership one year may be the result of extension growth coming of age. A daughter church may have developed to the place that it became a distinct, organized congregation. If this is true, the church probably did not really decline. It just continued to grow in two places. A little research on the daughter church may show that it has been growing at a faster rate than the mother. Using the same graph, those additional facts can be displayed. They will show how the mother church has experienced both expansion and extension growth at the same time (examine Figure 3).

II

The Percentage Test

The second test measures the rate of growth in a congregation. What is the ratio between growth and membership? It is obvious that when a church of 100 members adds 100 new members that is a far more significant achievement than when a church of 3,000 members adds 100 members. How do you measure the distinction between the two and make the distinction visible?

1. Begin by determining the Decadal Growth Rate (DGR). That is a very simple process. Find the differences between membership now and ten years ago. Divide that difference by the membership at the beginning of the decade. Change the decimal to a percentage, and you have your DGR.

Take the membership totals used in Figure 1. This church, which we will call Mother Church, with 140 resident members, grew to 240 resident members in ten years. Its DGR (240 − 140 = 100 ÷ 140) was 71.3%. This church will double in size in thirteen years if it is able to maintain its present DGR.

However, as was indicated in Figure 3, the membership totals did not tell the whole story. This church had planted a daughter church and had become involved in extension as well as expansion growth. What was the DGR when the membership figures had been properly refined? A church with 140 members grew (mother-daughter together) to 400. Its DGR (400 − 140 = 260 ÷ 140) 185.7%. Mother Church, engaging in both extension and expansion growth, actually doubled (check Figure 3) sometime before

91

the end of 1975, in less than eight years, and almost tripled in ten years.

But three big questions arise. What does this tell us? What if my church actually declined in the ten-year period? Finally, what if we don't have ten consecutive years of figures, or, to put it another way, what if my church is only eight years old?

In a nutshell the DGR tells us how many new people were added to the church per hundred *beginning members* in a ten year period. Its value is that it can be used in comparing the growth rates of equal periods in the life of the church and can be very useful in helping to see what kind of growth is required if we are to meet the goals that we set. For example, suppose Mother Church should decide that by 1987 it wanted to have 500 resident members within its fellowship. What DGR would that require?

$$500 - 240 = 260 \div 240 = 108.3\%$$

Five hundred may be a good attainable goal, but it demands growth at 37 percent higher rate than the achievements of the last decade.

Suppose members at Mother Church decided that since 100 members were added during the last ten years, they would attempt to add 150 members in the next ten years. That, too, might be a good goal. It even looks impressive. It is 50 percent more people than the previous decade. But when you put it to the percentage test, you will find it comes up short.

$$390 - 240 = 150 \div 240 = 62.5\%$$

It is almost a 10 percent lower DGR than in the previous ten years.

Now to the second question. If your church declined during the decade, the process for discovering the rate of decline is exactly the same as that for growth. But you figure *decadal decline rates* instead of DGR. Suppose your church had 1,000 members in 1967 and declined to 800 by 1977.

$$800 - 1,000 = -200 \div 1,000 = -20\%$$

Your church declined at the rate of 20 percent per decade.

What about the church that is only eight years old?

When you divide the net increase by the beginning membership, you do not have the *Decadal* Growth Rate. Rather, you have the *eight-year growth rate*. It tells you how many people were added to the church per hundred members in *eight* years. The two cannot be compared. For comparisons to have meaning they must be over the same period of time. Therefore, we must find a way to transpose an eight year (or any other period of time) growth rate to DGR or discover another method of comparison. Both processes are possible and useful.

To discover what the DGR would be if the same growth rate continued for ten years is a simple arithmetic process. Take an imaginary church that began with 100 members in 1970 and had 350 members at the end of 1975. What would be the DGR for that five year period?

1. Find difference between ending and beginning membership: 350 − 100 = 250.

2. Divide difference by beginning membership: 250 ÷ 100 = 250%.

3. Divide period growth rate by number of years in period: 250 ÷ 5 = 50%.

4. Multiply that quotient by 10: 50 × 10 = 500% DGR.

While the above process is simple, the DGR has some limitations. It only takes into consideration growth based on beginning membership. It does not take into consideration those that come in each of the ten years of the decade. In addition to the DGR we need to find another more accurate basis of comparison. To do this go to step two of the percentage test.

2. Compute the Annual Average Growth Rate (AAGR). Do this even if you have ten years of figures. Please note, however, *you do not get the AAGR by dividing the growth rate you have (whether for ten years, eight years, or fifteen years) by the number of years involved.*

Read that last sentence again! It seems that the simple procedure would be to divide the DGR by ten or if your growth rate figure is for eight years, to divide by eight. *But that method is wrong!* Suppose your church had fifty members and in three years had grown to 100 members. Obviously the growth rate for three years is 100 percent.

$$100 - 50 = 50 \div 50 = 100\%$$

It would appear that the AAGR would be 33.3 percent (100% ÷ 3 = 33.3%). Not so! Lets check it out.

Beginning Membership	50
GR 1st Year	.333
New members 1st year	16.6
Membership end 1st year (50 + 16.6)	66.6
GR 2nd year	.333
New members 2nd year	22.2
Membership end 2nd year (66.6 + 22.2)	88.8
GR 3rd Year	.333
New members 3rd year	29.3
Membership end 3rd year (88.8 + 29.3)	108.1

In three years, at 33.3 percent each year, you would have climbed well above 100 members. The reason this way of computing AAGR does not work is because the DGR tells how many were added per hundred beginning members. The AAGR must take into consideration the new members that have been added each year. It must tell how many new members were added per hundred members in one year while the total membership changes each year.

To figure the AAGR is a complicated process.[4] Rather than go into details of that process, Table I had been added at the end of this chapter. Find the ratio between the ending (e) and beginning (b) membership of your church for the years under study. Do this by dividing the former by the latter (e/b). To illustrate, look at Mother Church again (Figure 1). In this example, the ratio is 1.7 ($240 \div 140 = 1.7$). Ending membership (e) is 1.7 larger than beginning membership (b). Now turn to Table I. Locate the e/b ratio for your church (or the nearest figure to it) down the left-hand column. Now find the correct number of years involved by looking across the top of the table. Where these two columns (e/b ratio across, year down) converge, you will find your AAGR.

If you are working with more than ten years, we suggest you divide your data into ten year periods, as far as possible, and then figure the DGR and AAGR for each section.

The AAGR can be projected across a simple graph through any number of years (examine Figure 4). It, therefore, becomes extremely valuable in showing where a church will be in five or ten years if it continues at the same AAGR. If Mother Church wanted to grow for twenty years at the rate it did between 1967 and 1973, that could be projected also. The growth facts of Mother Church for these years are: $260 - 140 = 120 \div 140$ = 85.7 percent six year growth rate. DGR for this six years is 143 percent. The AAGR is 10.9 percent.

Look at Figure 4 again. The AAGR makes it possible to compare unequal growth periods equally and accurately. It, therefore, makes it possible to compare the growth rates of certain sections of a larger period under study. It also will enable you to compare the growth of your church to the growth of other churches in a meaningful way. Finally, it will enable you to compare the growth of your church to the population growth of your community.

Using census information,[5] find how much the population of your community has grown or declined in the last decade. Using that information calculate the AAGR of the population. Compare that to the growth of your church. You may find:

(1) That your church has grown while the community has lost population. That is a sign of growth health.

(2) That your church has declined while your community has grown. This is the sign of serious growth sickness.

(3) That your church has grown at about the same rate as your community. That is a sign of mere maintenance ministries with no penetration of the unchurched community.

(4) That your church has remained static in a declining population. That is a sign of some growth vigor.

(5) That your church has remained static in a growing population. That is also a sign of growth sickness.

The AAGR makes this sort of instructive comparison a possibility.

3. Compute the annual growth rate (AGR) for each of the years under study.[6] To do this the net increase (or decline) must be computed for each year. Then, the net increase must be divided by the membership at the beginning of the year. The resulting percentage is the AGR. Let's look at Mother Church again.

Figure 4

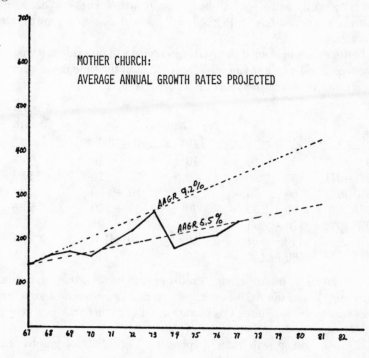

Years	Membership	Net Gain Loss	Computation	Annual Growth Rate
1968-1967	160 − 140 =	20	20 ÷ 140	14.3%
1969-1968	170 − 160 =	10	10 ÷ 160	6.3%
1970-1969	160 − 170 =	−10	−10 ÷ 170	− 5.9%
1971-1970	190 − 160 =	30	30 ÷ 160	18.8%
1972-1971	220 − 190 =	30	30 ÷ 190	15.9%
1973-1972	260 − 220 =	40	40 ÷ 220	18.2%
1974-1973	180 − 260 =	−80	−80 ÷ 260	−30.8%
1975-1974	200 − 180 =	20	20 ÷ 180	11.1%
1976-1975	210 − 200 =	10	10 ÷ 200	5.0%
1977-1976	240 − 210 =	30	30 ÷ 210	9.5%

In this particular church there is no sustained pattern of growth or decline. Just by looking at the AGR figures, one can determine that growth has been sporadic. On the graph (Figure 3), expansion growth appears to be consistent, if not spectacular. The primary value of growth rates is to clarify actual growth-health or growth-sickness. What actual numerical growth and a simple graph will not reveal, annual growth rates make clear.

A better example of what the AGR can reveal will be evident if we look at the record of Daughter Church (Figure 3) from the time it was planted (1970) until the end of the years under study (1977).

Years	Membership	Net Gain Loss	Computation	Annual Growth Rate
1971-1970	20 − 10 =	10	10 ÷ 10	100%
1972-1971	50 − 20 =	30	30 ÷ 20	150%
1973-1972	60 − 50 =	10	10 ÷ 50	20%
1974-1973	90 − 60 =	30	30 ÷ 60	50%
1975-1974	110 − 90 =	20	20 ÷ 90	22.2%
1976-1975	140 − 110 =	30	30 ÷ 110	27.3%
1977-1976	160 − 140 =	20	20 ÷ 140	14.3%

What looks like, and is, strong, healthy growth is, nevertheless, becoming anemic. When the AGR begins a steep decline, numerical growth is almost sure to follow. To see this picture vividly, go on to the next step of the percentage test.

4. Display the growth rates graphically. Two kinds of graphs lend

themselves to objectifying growth rate facts.

First, use a tool prepared especially to show *rate of increase and decline* called semilogarithmic graph paper. You may be unfamiliar with semilog paper and its properties. It can be secured at most stores which handle drafting and blueprint supplies. If you cannot locate a supply, you can prepare your own.[7] We will not go into an explanation of logarithmic principles or a description of why this instrument is able to objectify the results of the percentage test. It will be sufficient to say that semilogarithmic graph paper differs from simple graph paper in two important ways. (As you read these two distinctions, look at the samples of semilog graph paper in Figure 5.)

a. It has a special logarithmic *vertical* scale. The horizontal scale, which indicates *time*, is marked exactly as on a simple graph. But the vertical scale, which indicates *size*, is graduated. Each unit gets progressively smaller as it moves up the axis.

b. The vertical scale is arranged in a series of cycles. Each one of these divisions is increased one digit. The first begins with 1 (not zero), the second with 10, the third with 100, the fourth with 1,000, the fifth with 10,000, and so on. For use in measuring growth rates of single congregations, three cycle semilog paper is more than sufficient.

Now, with this minimal explanation, using a sheet of semilog paper, graph the growth of your church over the past decade. (See Figure 6.) *Use membership figures, not AGR figures. The semilog graph uses actual membership totals, but objectifies rate of growth.* Mark the years along the horizontal scale. Mark the vertical scale according to the beginning size of your church. If the beginning membership was less than ten, begin with one in the first cycle. If beginning membership was between ten and 100, begin with ten in the first cycle, etc. Note the various possibilities in Figure 5.

When you have located annual membership figures on the graph with a dot and connected each with a line, lay the simple graph you did earlier alongside this graph. How does the growth of your church look now? Would you characterize it as healthy? What observations would you make? Write them down! They will become important when you begin to finalize your diagnosis.

The semilog graph presents its most dramatic picture with large figures. It is especially useful in graphing the growth of synods, conferences, associations, and conventions of churches over several years. If your church growth was confined to only one cycle, the contrast may not be as vivid. You need to move on to the next type of graph.

Figure 5

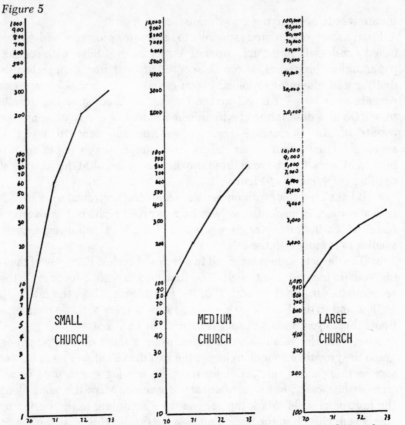

The second type of graph that lends itself to showing rates of growth is a bar graph.[8] To develop this graph go back to simple graph paper. In the center of the sheet draw a horizontal axis. Remember that positive values are always indicated above the axis and negative values are indicated below the axis. Begin by marking off the years exactly as you did on the horizontal axis in the other two graphs.

To determine your vertical scales, study the annual growth rates you prepared on each of the years under study. Your vertical scale must be marked so as to accommodate the extremes of annual growth rate and annual growth decline. For example, Mother Church varied from an AGR of 18.8 percent to an annual decline rate (ADR) of −30.8 percent. (See Figure 7.) Daughter Church's scale must vary from 150 percent to 14.3 percent. (See Figure 8.) Plot the AGR's of your church on this graph and outline boldly each bar or column, so that it stands out in bold relief. You

Figure 6

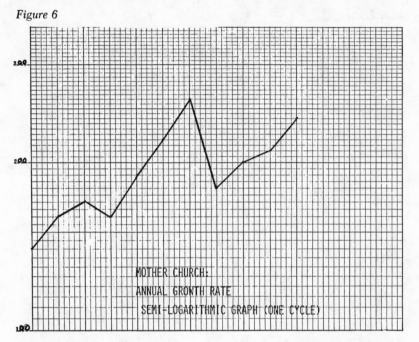

MOTHER CHURCH:
ANNUAL GROWTH RATE
SEMI-LOGARITHMIC GRAPH (ONE CYCLE)

may want to use colors.

To explicitly contrast AGR's to simple numerical growth engage in one more graphic exercise. Impose the graph of numerical growth over your bar graph of AGR. Look at Figure 9, which does this for Mother Church.

5. The final step in the percentage test is an exercise in comparisons. Let me suggest three. Using your semilog graph, compare your AGR to your AAGR. How? Make a second semilog graph exactly as the first. Then project your AAGR as a straight line running from the beginning membership point to the ending membership point. *A straight line on semilog graph paper always indicates a constant rate of growth.* Your AAGR is a constant rate of growth. Now, using the two lines, note what years you did better than average and what years your growth was below average. Can you explain why either was true? Were you just lucky some years? Was God only willing to bless you some years? There are other explanations, and those answers are what you look for in a diagnosis of the growth health of a church.

Using the same graph, project the growth of your church if it had maintained the same AAGR (or AADR) as the population. You figured the AAGR for the population of your community earlier. To explain this

Figure 7

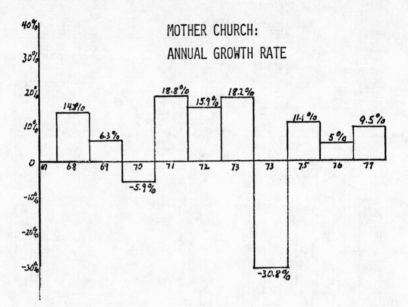

MOTHER CHURCH:
ANNUAL GROWTH RATE

Figure 8

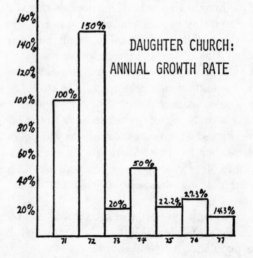

DAUGHTER CHURCH:
ANNUAL GROWTH RATE

Figure 9

b b328

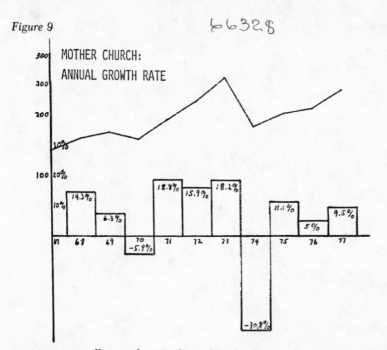

MOTHER CHURCH:
ANNUAL GROWTH RATE

process, we will consider Mother Church again and inform you that this congregation was located in a community growing at the AAGR of 5 percent. To project this on your semi-log graph do these things (see Figure 10).

1. Multiply the beginning membership by AAGR of the population ($140 \times 5\% = 7$).
2. Add product to beginning membership ($140 + 7 = 147$).
3. Locate new membership on semilog graph with a dot.
4. Extend a line from beginning membership point, through the new dot, to the line of the last year under study.

Study this comparison carefully. What does it tell you about the growth health of your church?

Finally, it has been discovered through research that the biological growth rate of a congregation is about 25 percent per decade. That is an AAGR of about 2.2 percent. Using the same procedure as above, project the growth of your church if it had only baptized the children of its members. Compare that line to the AAGR of your church. What does this comparison say about your church's growth?

Figure 10

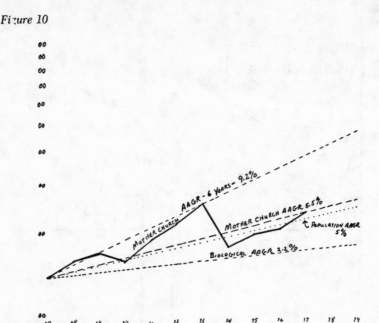

Observations:

1. Mother Church did, between 1967-1969 and 1970-1973, grow at a rate greater than the AAGR. During the last three years it has been below the AAGR.

2. Mother Church's AAGR has barely exceeded the AAGR of the population.

3. While Mother Church has grown faster than the biological growth rate, it has not significantly exceeded that growth factor.

III

The Body Count Tests

The third test measures the *kind* of growth a church has experienced. If churches only grow three ways (biologically, by transfer, and by conversions from the world), just how has your church been growing?

1. The process involved in making this test is simple: you must count bodies for at least the last five years! But many churches do not distinguish biological growth from conversion growth. They are all lumped into one group, since all would be admitted through baptism. Also, some

churches hold very strictly to the immersion of believers as the only proper mode of New Testament baptism. They would, therefore, require any person, however long a Christian, who might become a member of their church from another denominational group to be so baptized. This person is properly a part of the transfer growth of that church and should be so counted.

Because of these complications, it is necessary to be most careful at this point. It is best to go through the list of new members for each of the last five years and definitely identify each one as he was added to the church. Is he biological, transfer, or conversion growth?

When this task is completed, you will have four figures for each year:

a. The total minor children of members added through baptism or confirmation;

b. The total number won to Christ somewhere else, but added to the congregation by letter of recommendation, restoration, or as Christians coming from other churches through baptism;

c. the total number converted to Christ and baptized from the unchurched community; and

d. the total additions for the year, the sum of the first three.

2. Proceed to the second body count test. It is just as important to know how a church has lost members as to know how it has gained them. Just as there are only three ways a church can grow, there are only three ways that a church can lose members: death, transfer, or "reversion."

Death and transfer we readily understand. But we are not really clear on what "reversion" means. Do church members really "revert" and, if so, what constitutes reversion? For the purposes of this diagnosis, we suggest three groups that might be considered reversions.

a. Members who, by action of the congregation or church judicial body, have been excluded from the church

b. Members who live in open rebellion against Christ and his church and count themselves as outsiders, part of the world away from Christ

c. Members who have been nonresident at least one year without becoming part of another church

These, too, must be counted for the past five years. Again, you may come up with four different figures, one total for each of the three ways members may be lost to the church and a figure that is the sum of all of these.

3. Prepare a bar graph that will make obvious the facts you have discovered. In the center of a sheet of simple graph paper, draw a horizontal axis. Develop a bar graph exactly as you did in the percentage

test. The column above the axis will show total new members in each year. That column should be divided into three sections showing accurately the number added through biological, transfer, and conversion growth. The column below the axis will show the total members lost. It, too, may be divided into three sections, accurately depicting the number lost through death, transfer, and reversion.

Study Figure 11. This is a graph prepared by the Vale Street Baptist Church, Bloomington, Illinois. This church was also involved in extension growth. In 1973, their "mission" became the College Avenue Baptist Church, Normal, Illinois. The transfer of fifty-five members to that new church has been set apart from other transfer losses. They have properly

Figure 11

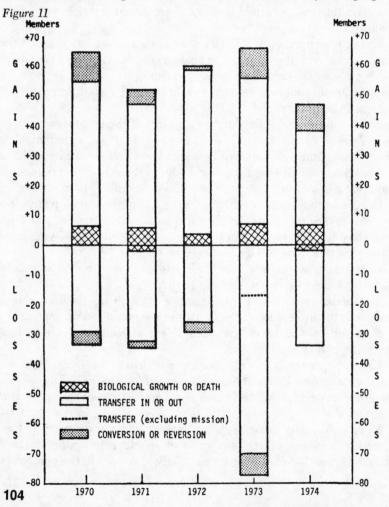

refined their figures.

Quite apart from the new church, it is obvious that most of the growth of this church has been transfer growth. This is the pattern in many churches. How about your own? How has your church been gaining and losing members? To improve the situation, what kind of strategy is required?

IV

The Geographical Test

Another examination, from a different perspective, to be administered to a church by a growth diagnostician may be called the geographical test. It answers the question, where do our new members come from?

By this question, no reference is intended to the national or regional origin of individuals. The purpose is not to pinpoint ethnicity or isolate sectionalism, as valuable as that may be. The question we seek to answer is simple. Where did members added to the church during the past five years actually live in reference to the principal meeting place of the church at the time they became members?

This question raises another question. What possible value does that information have for the matter of growth? What can it tell us about the growth health of a church?

The value of this test is that it reveals vividly those areas of a community that are presently the focus of growth ministries. At the same time, it will boldly call attention to geographical areas that are being neglected. Very often, when this study has been completed and objectified, it illustrates that not only the racial and language culture people are being overlooked, but also that socioeconomic people-units are being ignored. Housing in America continues to reflect the racial, cultural and socioeconomic configuration of a community. The geographical tests usually indicate whether or not your church is really addressing your message to the entire community or only to some of its geographical sectors.

These observations do not suggest, necessarily, that the most effective way to share Christ in these different housing sectors is through expansion growth strategies. Perhaps extension or bridging growth techniques are demanded.

The purpose of the test is to show those geographical areas where a church's ministries have been directed and effective in contrast to those areas which have been ignored or neglected or in which ministries have been ineffective.

How do you go about making this test?

1. On a large map of your church community locate the actual place of residence for all those people who have been added to your church membership during the past five years. If people travel significant distances to worship with your church, it may be necessary to use two maps. The first should be an enlarged map of the immediate community where your church meets. This would enable you to identify every subdivision and street. The second map should chart the larger metropolitan or county area. On it you could locate those newer members who travel from beyond your immediate community.

2. Use a distinctive mark for each of the five years. In this manner you will be able to see clearly growth effectiveness on an annual basis as well as for the entire five year period.

Very often the geographical test indicates clearly that the major outreach efforts of a church are being directed almost exclusively toward new arrivals in the larger community. The homes of new members will be located predominately in new subdivisions, perhaps not even in the near vicinity of the church building.

New arrivals are usually a responsive segment of the population. But giving primary attention to these groups usually means that most growth comes by transfer.

3. Analyze the findings of the test. To do this, answer these questions.

a. What specific geographical areas have we neglected and in what areas has our ministry been ineffective?

b. What geographical areas have been responsive and what has been our ministry in them?

c. What are the social characteristics of these different geographical areas?

d. Why has our ministry been effective or ineffective?

e. What factors have caused us to neglect certain geographical areas?

f. Where are these areas located in reference to the church building?

g. How can we improve our ministry in areas from which we have drawn growth?

h. What kind of ministries can we begin that will be evangelistically effective in areas where we have been inactive or ineffective?

V

The Leadership Test

Leadership imbalance has been identified as one of the major hindrances to a growing church. No church can grow that does not have volunteer leaders whose major ministry is toward the unchurched community. A survey of the leadership of your church will enable you to draw a profile that will describe accurately the present growth situation in your church.

1. List every office, position, or leadership role in your church and the person who fills it.[9] If an individual fills more than one role, list each role and that individual beside each office he holds.

2. In addition to these names, list those persons who actually serve in unelected posts of leadership. You may have a group of men and women who visit the aged each week as an expression of their ministry to Christ. You may have ten women that visit absentees every Thursday morning. There may be a group of men and women who are involved in a program of personal evangelism each week without holding elected offices. Add each of those to your list. Note the nature of each individual's ministry beside his name.

3. Classify each position. Is the function of that position primarily for those who are already in the church? Is the purpose of the position to touch the unenlisted Christian and the nonbeliever with Jesus Christ? How is the person filling the role, actually performing in that position? Weigh each office. Mark those whose ministry is aimed primarily at building up those already in the church with "A." Identify those whose ministry is aimed primarily at those outside the church with "B."

4. List all partially salaried leaders in your church. Classify each of them with a small "a" or "b" according to their principle ministry. Compile the names of all fully salaried leaders in your church. Classify each of them (with small letters) according to his primary ministry. Finally, make a list of state or national church leaders who may be in the membership of your church.

5. Tally the various leadership groups into five groups. We will consider Mother Church as an example. In that church the tally went like this:

a. Volunteer leaders ministering to church members: 82
b. Volunteer leaders ministering to unchurched community: 6
c. Partially salaried leaders (both "a"):   2

d. Fully salaried leaders (one "a," two "b"): and   3

e. Leaders of larger church (neither "a" nor "b"):   2

Is there any evidence of imbalance at this point?

6. Using simple graph paper, prepare a leadership profile of your church. In essence, this is another bar graph. Draw your axis near the bottom of the paper. It should provide for five columns. Identify each column as volunteer leader I (VL-I), volunteer leaders II (VL-II), partially salaried leaders (PSL), fully salaried leader (FSL), and denominational and other leaders (DOL). Determine your vertical scale so that it will accommodate the largest group in the survey. Examine Figure 12, which is a leadership profile for Mother Church, as an example of how your church's profile might look. Then use Figure 12 for a little exercise in analyzation. After looking at this profile, how would you answer these three questions:

a. Can this church grow significantly if it maintains this leadership balance?

b. Why or why not?

Figure 12

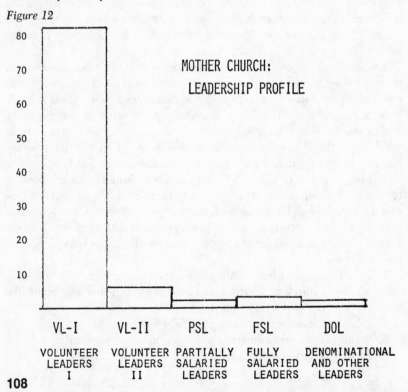

c. What must happen if Mother Church is to have a significant growth pattern in the years ahead?

A few committed outreach people and two fully salaried staff members concentrating on reaching non-Christians can do wonders. But this church cannot grow significantly until VLII's are multiplied. For significant growth special attention needs to be given to multiplying and equipping VLII individuals for their ministry in the world. Steadfastly refuse the temptation to shift them to VLI status.

VI

The Time Use Test

We are all aware that time is a very special commodity. It is the "stuff" from which life is made. It may be squandered or spent but it cannot be saved up or hoarded. All of us, if we live, will have an equal amount of time today. There will be twenty-four hours, or 1,440 minutes, or 86,400 seconds, however you wish to count it. No one will have more or less. Beyond this, the Bible makes clear that God is concerned that we make the most of our time (Eph. 5:16; Col. 4:5).

Obviously church members do not have *unlimited* time for involvement in the ministries of the church. No one can stretch a day into thirty hours. In the twenty-four hours each person must sleep, eat, work, relax, and perform household duties. In a given week the average church member has only a few hours to give to his church. Knowing this, it becomes extremely important that we make meetings count.

One of the factors that retards church growth is the misuse of valuable, irretrievable, limited man-hours. If few of those hours are invested in solving growth problems and in performing growth ministries, the church cannot expect to grow.

An important question for the church growth diagnostician is, How is time being spent? How are the limited hours of both volunteer leaders and salaried leaders being invested?

There is a very simple method for determining if time misuse is a problem in the growth of your church.

1. Do a time analysis of the various meetings of decision making groups in your congregation. Find out whether growth is in reality a priority for the church. If it is, it will show up in the investment of time. If we are not devoting time to church growth, all the attestations that can be mustered will not make church growth a priority. We invest our time in that which is really most important to us (or else we come apart at the seams).

109

2. The process is very simple. Ask someone to meet with the various boards and committees of the church for at least two regular meetings. The person need not interfere with the regular agenda. The meeting should go on as usual. The visitor should note the time spent on various subjects.[10] Divide a three hour meeting period into twelve, fifteen-minute segments. The matters under discussion during each of those segments can be easily recorded.

3. When this has been completed, classify and tally the findings. How much time in the meeting was actually given to dealing with growth problems? You will discover very quickly the number one priority of church leadership in this process. What gets major time investment?

4. Finally, ask the fully salaried and partially salaried personnel to make an analysis of their own time use for three or four weeks. Time should be given on Saturday or Sunday afternoon for each to write down his goals for the following week. What does he actually hope to accomplish during the seven days ahead? On a prepared form, let him keep a record of how his time was spent by fifteen-minute segments.[11]

This process may sound like a big chore, but it actually can be done with very little effort. This exercise is prerequisite to improving your time management skills. Furthermore, it will tell the person attempting to diagnose the growth health of a church how much time is being given by salaried leaders to growth matters. If the pastor is never able to give time to evangelism and enlistment, it is unlikely that others in the congregation will so invest their time.

An analysis of the goals spelled out for each week will also prove helpful. How important are growth objectives in the weekly goals of the employed staff?

Recapitulation

These seven tests, when carried out with accuracy and analyzed carefully, will expose no-growth illness. Compiling them with precision and interpreting them with care is very important. Here again are the seven questions that must be answered:

1. Has the church been growing?
2. At what rate has church growth occurred?
3. How has the church been adding members?
4. How has the church been losing members?
5. Where do new members come from?
6. What kind of leaders do we have?
7. How do we spend our time?

6
Sharing the Church Growth Data

THE CHURCH GROWTH WEEKEND

The Perspective of the Weekend

The Church Growth Weekend is a time for commitment. It takes courage to make a commitment. This commitment need not be blind or unplanned. It can focus on need and measureable goals.

Accurate data is absolutely essential for planning church growth strategies. The Church Growth Weekend provides an opportunity for key leaders in the church to spend time studying accurate data indicating what a church has done, what it is doing and what it could do. No church can select spiritual priorities without accurate data.

The stimulation from this study creates hostility, awareness, dissatisfaction, determination, and concern. These are integral elements in a climate appropriate for church growth. It is from this climate new directions are charted. Goal ownership becomes a reality for more than the paid leadership.

The twelve hours of a Church Growth Weekend can change the lifestyle of a church for the future. Needs will come into focus that were never so prominent before. And, needs are the launching pads for church growth today.

The weekend moves from learning the concepts and theories of church growth to the concrete application of those concepts and theories. Church growth as it is generally experienced in a variety of situations will be brought to focus on what can and should happen in one particular setting. An analysis of data will lead to appropriate action plans that will affect the thought, life, and behavior of a particular church.

The following diagram is a simplification of the process of the Church Growth Weekend.

The Details of the Weekend

Who Should Be There? Key leaders in a church can best be determined by a pastor. The people who attend should represent a cross section of the

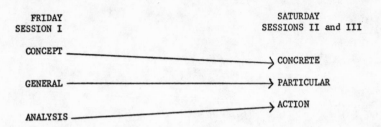

```
FRIDAY                                    SATURDAY
SESSION I                              SESSIONS II and III

CONCEPT  ─────────────────────────────→ CONCRETE

GENERAL  ─────────────────────────────→ PARTICULAR

                                      ─→ ACTION
ANALYSIS ─────────────────────────────
```

church's family. No one group should dominate the participants. A cultural, age, economic, and interest "mix" is very important to the ultimate success of the weekend. Newer church members should have some representation.

This meeting calls for the responses from people who are generally positive in nature.

It would be unusual if anyone under the age of seventeen would want to attend due to the length and nature of the sessions.

Invitations to the meeting should be extended by the pastor. This is not designed for a large, congregational-type experience. Every effort should be made to clearly state the purpose of the sessions in order to avoid a negative reaction from the church body at large.

Session I (First day, Friday, three to four hours)

Focus #1: The efforts in this session will focus on creating an awareness of church growth in concept and theory. There are films designed for this. These are spiritual, attractive, professional, inspirational, and present the basic foundation for understanding church growth. New terminology must be introduced in most settings. Illustrations that clarify the meanings of those new terms can be provided through the video medium. Broad, sweeping guidelines are needed to introduce information that is essential for understanding the data that will be presented later in the session.

Focus #2: Building the group for a spiritual encounter is important. This is more than a spiritual "pep rally." From this experience lives will be refocused to new spiritual priorities. It is important that a receptive and positive climate be prepared for the data-sharing time. This may be one value for having an outside consultant as a leader for the weekend.

Focus #3: A lecture is to be presented on "Limitations to Church Growth." What actually hinders church growth? A careful analysis of hindrances or limitations will be led by one of the leaders for the weekend. There are thousands of churches which are not growing in America today. There are some reasons why. These reasons can be discovered. These reasons occur over and over again in various situations. A look at these reasons will usually point out the existence of at least one in the church in which the weekend retreat is being experienced. This lecture is basically negative in tone, but is the foundation for a positive answer to come in a later lecture entitled, "Marks of a Growing Church."

Focus #4: The research or data study comes after the proper climate has been prepared. Twelve weeks of preparation should have produced accurate, attractive, and clearly illustrated data. Proper communication of the data is crucial. The pastor should present the data on the past and present profile of the church. A suggested pattern of presentation is:

* Where have our members come from? (Geographical study)
* Has our church been growing? (Membership study)
* What kind of growth has our church been experiencing?
      (Biological)   (Transfer)   (Conversion)
* How have we lost members from our church?
* Analysis of church leadership and time management.
   (What kind of leadership do we have?)
   (How do we use our time?)

A look at this data will create the discussion which will be the basis for the rest of the weekend. It will probably exhaust the remaining amount of time allotted for Session I.

Reminder: Take your time in Session I. It takes time for people to absorb this much material.

Session II (Second day, Saturday, four hours)

Focus #1: Creative activities should begin this session. A motivational tape or film should be used to create a climate of enthusiasm. Group dynamics and building relationships will be necessary for working through the information that will lead to goal setting. Positive enthusiasm is the proper climate for learning the principles of church growth.

Focus #2: A lecture on "Marks of a Growing Church" is to lead the thinking during this session. The climate of church growth is enthusiasm, the content is based on principles. This lecture gives some positive answers to the lecture on "What Hinders Church Growth?" from Session I. Characteristics that form basic principles of church growth will be the focus of this lecture and these will be applied to the local experience at hand.

Focus #3: Small groups should be assigned specific data to study. Discussion should center around "when" these statistics were made, "what" were the existing conditions, "what" does this mean for those in this church today, and "where" do we go from here? A suggested way to assign the specific growth profiles would be:

Group   I: "Where have our members come from?" (Geographic study); "How have we lost members from our church?"

Group II: "Has our church been growing?"
"What kind of growth has our church been experiencing?" (Study resident, nonresident, biological, transfer, conversion, and growth statistics.)

Group III: "Analysis of church leadership and time management." (What kind of leaders do we have and how are we using our time?)

A report should be brought from each group. Open discussion should be allowed and new ideas recorded.

Focus #4: Each of the small groups should reconvene to plan what the church could do to influence in a positive manner the area of their statistical study. Planning for the next three months (1-3) should be in detail. Months 4-8 should be planned in a more general way. Months 9-14 should focus on broad plans. A second church growth weekend should be planned and scheduled for a weekend during the fourteenth month.

In each of these time frames growth strategies should have priority attention. Carefully worded purpose statements should be hammered out that will establish the guidelines for each strategy and each time segment. Measureable goals should be set for each strategy and time segment.

A detailed calendar for months 1-3 should be designed.

1. A specific date should be set aside for planning in detail months 4-8.
2. Measureable goals should be set.
3. Nonmeasureable goals should be set.
4. Possible assignment suggestions planned.

Months 9-14 should be set up on the basis of broad calendar guidelines. A specific date should be set in the future for the detail planning of these months.

Every strategy plan and calendar date must be viewed with regard to its impact upon the church body. Unless the church body has given authority to this church growth weekend task force, no responsibility should be specifically assigned. The small groups should design ways to communicate the data and its implications. The data must be viewed from a spiritual perspective. Enthusiastic communication of these facts will be necessary if the church body is to respond in a positive manner.

Session III (Second day, Saturday, three hours)

Focus #1: A sharing time should allow each group to express its findings, strategies, and measureable goals. Undoubtedly nonmeasureable goals will have surfaced and these should be shared.

This sharing time should be recorded in writing and perhaps on cassette recording. A few new ideas will emerge that will need consideration. However, the purpose of the weekend must be kept in focus. *The plan is to look at growth patterns and how to bring about statistically measureable growth in the church.*

Focus #2: A definite decision should be made on a time and method for sharing the data and goals with the church body. The specific plans recommended by the weekend study group should be approved by the church body by formal voting. Goal ownership on the part of large numbers of church members will insure more interest and participation.

Focus #3: The closing activity is a lecture by the leader for the weekend. It is to present ways in which to create an atmosphere for growth in the church. The lecture is to include in its design motivational and inspirational materials that will challenge those present to "think church growth and plan church growth." A call for commitment should conclude the weekend. This call for prayer and commitment should be led by the pastor.

Summary

Church growth is a way of thinking, planning, and doing. It is not a program that is conducted once or twice per year. It is a way of life for the church.

This weekend is designed to bring to light needs from which plans for growth can emerge.

A church must commit to growth. Growth is not automatically achieved. It is not achieved apart from hard work. Growth is possible if accurate data is used for building an awareness of spiritual needs that a church must meet. This awareness must express itself in a careful selection of priorities, action plans, and allocation of resources.

The Church Growth Weekend is the beginning of the practical application of church growth principles as a way of life within a particular church.

7
Going on to Expansion Growth

"Growth is the only evidence of life."

Expansion Growth Requires an Expansion Growth Strategy

Recently Dr. George Peters stated: "During a conversation I asked Dr. Jerry Falwell of Lynchburg, Virginia, how they went about reaching so many with the gospel. His answer to me was classic, 'From the very beginning we prayed and prayed that God would give us the solid, absolute conviction that every man was reachable with the Gospel if we could only find the key to his heart.' " [1] This is the beginning point of expansion growth. The strategy must be designed for growth from outside the church.

Expansion growth strategy goes beyond vestibule visitation.

Fellowship in the life of a church is a theological issue. It is an integral part of life with Christ and his family the church. Warm, personal, friendly conversation is an important function of the church. Church activities that lead to deeper intrapersonal relationships within the church family are important priorities. Efforts to bring the unchurched into the church building or involve them in programs sponsored by the church are excellent means of outreach.

But, expansion growth strategy requires going beyond the vestibule, foyer and the stained-glass windows. The arena for expansion growth is outside the four walls of the church building. It goes beyond bringing unchurched persons to "our ball park where we make the rules, set the time frames and determine who is going to pitch the ball and make all the decisions."

Expansion growth is diagramed in chapter 1 in the following manner: When the church goes beyond its walls to reach people, one barrier, namely the stained-glass one, is crossed. This is called E_1 evangelism. There are times when this could be considered E_0 but the primary description of this strategy is E_1.

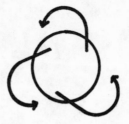

Many churches, in excellently accessible locations, have empty seats in classrooms and sanctuaries. People drive by in large numbers while the "Good News" is being shared inside the church. Thousands of them need this message in order to know how to respond to Jesus Christ as Savior, and continue on to responsible church membership. Others need to find the joy of renewed commitment to their faith in Christ. They will continue to drive by so long as the message and energies of that church continue to be focused inside the four walls.

Expansion growth demands that a church family decide it is time to tell the story of the love of God to someone else besides one another.

Expansion growth requires keeping biological growth in proper perspective. Biological growth alone leads to stagnation and decline.

Expansion growth is a commitment that must be made by at least 10 percent of the church leadership. The key leader of the church is the pastor. No church will go on to expansion growth if the pastor is in opposition to it.

Expansion growth takes place outside the church building and the fruits of this growth are revealed inside the church building.

Expansion growth accepts the fact of variety among the unreached.

Luke 15 records three parables shared by Jesus. He describes the condition most Evangelicals call "being lost." All three stories are illustrations of "lostness."

Illustrations of Variety Among the Unreached

Illustration one is the parable of a lost sheep sought by a seeking shepherd. The second illustration focuses on a lost coin of great value to the woman who lost it. The third is a story of a rebel son and how he was dealt with by his forgiving father. A lost sheep, a lost coin, and a lost son are major parts of the illustrations. Each of them displays a different variety or "kind" of lostness.

The lost sheep was not like the rebel son. He did not purposefully detach himself from the shepherd as a deliberate act. He was not lost from the flock by the neglect of the shepherd. He did not play hide and seek when the shepherd sought to find him. It took considerable effort to pick him up and carry him back to the safety of the fold.

The lost coin was not like the lost sheep or the lost son. The coin was not a rebel nor did it wander away from the crowd. It was much harder to find when it was lost. It had no ability to give off a sound to enhance its possibility of being found. Coins can be lost by neglect of the coin owner. Coins have a different value from sheep and rebel sons.

The lost rebel son was not like the lost sheep or the lost coin. In a rebellious frame of mind he demanded to be left alone. He refused the caring and sharing nature of his father. He deliberately chose a life that was lost from that of his father. He demanded all that it was his right to have.

These three stories are astounding insights into the fact of the variety of people who are not involved in a relationship and/or fellowship with Jesus Christ. They are not exhaustive descriptions of the infinite variety of unreached persons. But, the broad categories point out the vast differences between unreached "types" of people.

Wherever there are people, there are lost ones. Some are like the lost sheep, others are like the lost coin, and many are like the rebel son. These lost persons can be found among white Anglo-Saxons, Spanish-Americans, Polish, Rumanian, Assyrian, Asiatic, South Americans, and blacks.

This brings to focus the fact that unreached people are made up of a mosaic of personality types. Ralph Winter has said, "While there are 2.7 billion people who do not even call themselves Christians, over three-fourths of them are beyond the range of any kind of normal (or cultural-near-neighbor) evangelization by existing churches. By normal evangelism I do not mean what is normally now being done, I refer as well to all of those various kinds of evangelism which believers in presently existing congregations would be capable of launching without surmounting unusual barriers of language and social structure." [2]

We are not all alike even when we are lost from the plan of God for our lives. We may have been taught that we are, but it is not accurate. All lost persons are not alike.

Acceptance of the responsibility for reaching varieties of the unreached.

James L. Sullivan, past president of the Southern Baptist Convention, said, "When you're lost, you cannot go by inner feelings; you need someone outside yourself to give you direction." [3]

The New Testament specifically points out that the church has a responsibility corporately and individually to go on to expansion growth. "And you will be witnesses for me in Jerusalem, in all of Judea and Samaria, and to the ends of the earth" (Act 1:8, TEV). "Go, then, to all my peoples everywhere and make them disciples: baptize them in the name of the Father, the Son, and the Holy Spirit, and teach them to obey every thing I have commanded you" (Matt. 28:19–20, TEV). Responsibility to the unreached must go beyond the level of an assumption. There must be a basic conviction that we are to grow by reaching unreached people.

A commitment to conversion growth as a priority leads to the continuous acceptance of the responsibility to reach the many varieties of unreached persons. Biological and transfer growth are vital to church growth. But if they are allowed to dim our vision of the unreached multitudes, expansion growth will be negligible.

Churches must sense and respond to a divine mandate to help lost persons find Christ and become involved in his plans for their lives and his church. This mandate is not selective. The call is to reach out to "whosoever will" respond. Whether or not they are "our kind" does not define the limit of responsibility. Expansion growth compels the church to find a way to carry out the commission to make disciples in all stratas of the population.

This brings us face to face with the next reality of expansion growth. *Expansion growth is too complex for any one strategy.*

The starting point of any strategy is extremely important to its ultimate outcome. If meeting needs is the starting point then variety in strategy will be a natural outcome. If "how much it costs" is the starting point the variety in strategy will be restricted. If "we can't do that here" is the starting point, a single strategy with little or no faith dimension will be the outcome.

The fact is, there is no one strategy for expansion growth that is universally successful. The following are only stimulants to create new thought patterns for strategy. Some will only serve as reminders that may renew sagging efforts.

The Strategy of Soil Testing

Farming in America has become a rather sophisticated industry. Seed companies, fertilizer distributors, agricultural departments, and universities have devised all types of scientific ways to test soils for potential crop yields. They can determine the most successful hybrid of seed, the type and quantity of the crop to be grown in that soil.

Churches need to learn how to test soil. The soil being the community to which it is directing its ministry. A large metropolitan area in a Southern state was surveyed to determine how the people in this metroplex ranked their personal needs. The top five needs in that community were presented by the residents as follows:

1. Loneliness
2. Hopelessness
3. Purposelessness
4. Fear
5. Emptiness

Church leaders turned to an advertising company and indicated what they felt the gospel contained for the lives of people living in this metroplex. The ad company strategists indicated the products of the gospel were a perfect answer to the needs of the people.

Too often churches meet and decide in closed session what the needs of the community are with no input from the community at large. This strategy will not work.

As is indicated in the Southern metroplex, the gospel has answers to the needs, but those with needs are not coming to church to hear the answers. Far too often when they do attend there are language, cultural, and traditional barriers that keep them from hearing the meanings of the gospel message. Even more often they are not attending church, and have no intention of starting in the near future. But, in many churches the only strategy is, "here we are, come and listen." So, if the unreached continue to drive by, their needs continue to go unmet by the church. Because the church that indicates "here we are, come and listen," has only one strategy for reaching the unreached.

Find out why the majority of the people are ignoring the church. The answer is not totally found in theology, the Bible, economic data, sociological data, educational philosophies, and so forth. Man must be viewed as a "whole person." His spiritual life is only one of his concerns. Why he ignores it cannot be discovered by an outsider looking at his external behavior. He may not be able to give you a totally accurate answer as to why he will not allow a God orientation in his life, but he is certainly a valid resource for finding such an answer. He is most certainly as valid a resource as a church committee that does not know his name, age range, culture, language, traditions, or "gut level" needs.

Soil-testing to find the where and why of spiritual response is a valid and essential strategy for expansion growth. Soil testing can discover responsive areas. There are times when a given area awakens to a spiritual sensitivity. As Jesus indicated to Nicodemus, "Just as you can hear the wind but can't tell where it comes from or where it will go next, so it is with the Spirit. We do not know on whom he will next bestow this life from heaven" (John 3:8, TLB). When an area is responsive to the gospel, we should focus resources on that area. One family concerned with the spiritual dimensions of their lives can open doors to scores of families that have previously been unresponsive. Soil-testing can provide information that will not allow a possible responsive area to go unnoticed.

The Strategy of Harvest Evangelism

Let's continue with our agricultural analogy for one more strategy illustration. Churches have been known to attempt the following procedure in an effort to have a spiritual harvest that will expand the kingdom of God and their church memberships.

Step One: Plow and prepare the soil, sow the seed, cultivate away the weeds, bring in the harvest machine immediately following the plow, planter, and cultivator. They attempt to do this in a one step operation. In nine out of ten instances *it will not work.*

The harvest evangelism concept is:

Step One: Properly prepare the soil.

Church Activity: Touch a person's life at his point of need.

Step Two: Sow properly an abundant supply of seeds (more than enough for a good harvest).

Church Activity: Cards, letters, Bible study leaflets, gospel tracts, share New Testament.

Step Two and One Half: Pray for providential help.

Step Three: Cultivate away weeds and other alien influences that hinder the growth of the crop.

Church Activity: Visit personally, call by phone, personal letter, Bible study leaflet, generally keep in touch.

Step Three and One Half: Pray for more providential help and good influences to replace the bad ones.

Step Four: Watch for the right time to harvest. Be ready with the right laborers, machinery, and storage space.

Church Activity: Harvest revival, personal visit, seek personal commitment.

A definition for harvest evangelism is: "Implanting the Word of God in the minds of people, fostering the growth of the Word of God in the lives of people and seeking a life changing and continuous response to Jesus Christ as He is revealed in the Word of God." [4]

The Strategy of Open Enrollment

The open enrollment strategy is to enroll in a Bible study group anyone, any place, at any time that he/she will give you permission to do so. Thousands of people are being reached for Bible study throughout the nation with this simple method.

This plan is being used extensively by Southern Baptists with significant results. Churches with other denominational persuasions have also used this to a great advantage.

Many churches are enlarging their Bible study and Sunday School enrollments through this strategy. These churches are finding new people who may choose not to be enrolled, but would like to be considered potential prospects. In one area for every one new enrollee, ten prospective families or forty new people were discovered.

Expansion growth requires continuous efforts to find new people who are not involved in a church or are not giving attention to the spiritual dimension of their lives. This effort goes beyond the strategy of placing a sign in an obvious place to inform the community concerning the times of the services and the name and phone number of staff members.

The Strategy of Productive Prospecting

A church must be convinced that a supply of prospects is absolutely essential to expansion growth. These prospects will have a qualitative value that is natural to each of them. That is, not all are as likely to be responsive as others. So in this sense they can be termed "better prospects."

Many top salesmen use as a rule of thumb it takes six prospects on a list to have one, really good one. If this is true, a church needs approximately sixty prospects on the list in order to have ten good ones.

Productive prospecting involves finding and touching the lives of scores of people while realizing not all will be potential members for the church. Remember, the church is to take up the ministry of Jesus Christ to the world. That ministry is described by word and deed as a "servant ministry." We must keep asking, "Are we here to serve or to be served?"

Churches planning an expansion growth strategy must keep a continuous effort toward productive prospecting.

Where do we find productive prospects?

Answer #1: Among our friends, relatives and acquaintances
   * Our friends need a meaningful relationship to Christ, just as much as strangers.

* Our friends need a church in which to function as a responsible church member, it may as well be ours.
* Our obligation to our friends is to help them find the best in life. That is found in relationship with Jesus Christ and membership in a church.

This same series of statements can be made concerning our relatives and acquaintances.

Answer #2: When we enlarge our circle of natural contacts.

* Identify with proud moments in the lives of people within the community and in the community itself.

  Illustration: A young man in your community is selected for one of the military academies. Write him, affirm him, praise him. He is in the upper 3 percent of high school young people in America.

  Illustration: Your community plans a special occasion that is to celebrate a civic achievement. Get involved. Other people have areas of involvement they consider just as important as what goes on in your church.

* Identify with crisis moments in the lives of people and in the community itself.

  Illustration: A school bus tragedy claims the life of a child or more than one child. A letter of comfort should be shared by an Evangelical church in that community.

  Illustration: A community is struck by a natural disaster. The church should perform a "social-spiritual" ministry in the community. This should be more than a prayer meeting, but should include one, too.

* Get acquainted with newcomers. It is a difficult task to move. A friendly attitude is generally always welcome.

Answer #3: Develop our sphere of influence.

* Be involved in some positive activity in community life.
* Be a booster of the good in the community.
* Have a desire to want to qualify as a caring church by exhibiting a caring spirit.
* Get to know people who know people.
* Everyone has a sphere of influence. Every person you get to know you will influence in some way and vice versa. When you have influence with him, you have influence with those to whom he relates as his sphere of influence. (See Appendix Exhibit #B for form that could be useful for this.)

Answer #4: In the people you meet in everyday life.

* Those you bump into at the grocery store, coffee shop, bus stop, Little League ball games, service station, and so on.
* Many of these do not touch your life by accident, but by design.
* Be alert to all types of possible ministries.
* Not everyone with whom you deal has to be responsive at first. Remember in your own life how you were touched by someone who cared, but had no idea you would ultimately respond to Christ and church membership.

The Strategy of Stopping and Starting

It is not unusual for a church to assume all it has to do to start growing is to simply start growing.

What a church can fail to recognize is the need to stop the decline and then start the growth. These can be two separate phases of the growth program.

Expansion growth may require at the outset a strategy to level off the decline of the data profile of the church.

The mixture of factors that may cause the decline may be of such nature that it cannot be reversed by one strategy. One factor may need to be isolated. This may be the factor that has created a nongrowth influence. Another factor may be discovered that is neither positively nor negatively contributing to the statistical profile of the church. Still another factor may be found to be a radical deterrent to growth. The influence of each of these factors may have to be neutralized before growth factors can be added to the mixture.

It is not safe to conclude that all growth factors are the exact opposite of nongrowth factors. A church can take each of its nongrowth factors and activate the growth factor that is its obvious opposite and this will not guarantee expansion growth. There may be a time when the decline of a church must be stopped and follow this with a strategy for growth.

Expansion growth faces the reality of communication gaps.

Someone once said, "words don't have meanings, only people have meanings." No matter how accurately the gospel is presented, someone who hears it will misunderstand some of the message. A church can be theologically accurate, doctrinally sound, and exhibit a very orthodox behavior pattern to the community. This does not guarantee the message and mission of that church will be received and understood by the community as a whole, nor its individual members.

People hear words or meanings that were not spoken nor shared. Idiomatic expressions which are common to a church may be foreign to the community. Hymns that meet the needs of the saints who have known and served for years, may communicate nothing to others. Sermons directed towards the unreached may totally miss the area of sensitivity in the community.

Churches must face the hard reality. Communication gaps occur in spiritual efforts just as in many others considered less sacred. Efforts toward expansion growth often bring a "head on collision" between the church and the unreached members of the community.

We may give off spiritual signals with the most godly theology and out of the purest motivation and the community not be tuned to our spiritual frequency. This is not because we are all right and they are all wrong. Not at all is this true. It may be that closing the communication gap must precede closing of the spiritual gap.

A Strategy for Communication

When the church embarks on a strategy for expansion growth, it must plan a communication strategy. Let us examine a communication model.

Regardless of how spiritually minded the church, by the time the message travels from the sender to the receiver many shades of meaning may come from the message. Unless the traditions and culture of the sender are identical, or nearly identical to the receiver, there will be a communication gap. The receiver will hear meanings the sender did not intend.

If the sender is preaching, the words he selects will trigger certain meaning responses in the receiver. The manner in which he gestures will convey meaning. The amount of emotion and emphasis on certain words creates another meaning context.

If the sender of the message uses the printed page another communication context arises. The reading age level of the receivers must be considered. A gospel tract must be as readable and attractive as it is theologically accurate. A printed brochure must be carefully planned in order for the receiver to be the major focus of it.

If the sender uses radio as the method for sending the message another communication strategy must be considered. Who is listening to the radio station being used? What is the age range, socioeconomic structure, educational level of those listening at the time of day the sender is sharing the message?

If the sender uses television to communicate to the receiver, another new communication strategy arises.

The gospel message can be shrouded in a communication fog. This fog can be created by:

* The person who is sending the message
* The words used to share the meaning of the message
* The methods used to share the message
* The cultural and traditional gaps between the sender and receiver

The gospel is too much "good news" to allow an improper communication strategy to blunt its penetration into the market place of twentieth-century life.

Plan all communication strategy with the need of the receiver as the number one focus of the plan. This does not diminish the reality of the Christ who stands behind the message to validate it. This does not mean the theological stance of the church has to be compromised. It is merely following the patterns of Christ who used all kinds of communication tools to share the message of the "good news." Fishermen, farmers, seamstresses, poor, rich, religious, nonreligious, lawyers, soldiers, builders, shepherds, children were all a focus of this message at one time or another.

Expansion Growth Requires an Expanding Church Staff

Thousands of churches across America are termed "one staff" churches. This may be a misnomer as we will discover later. It is probably more accurate to say these have only one paid or partially paid staff member. There is a need for churches to consider other persons within the church as potential staff members or ministers. Gifted lay persons can be used for a variety of tasks of the church.

Many of these thousands of churches are coming to face the truth about expansion growth—no one man can do it all.

The church is more than a one-man operation.

The law of stimulus and response comes into focus at this point. Remember every response is triggered by a stimulus. And certain stimuli gain certain responses.

The one staff church tends to have only one key stimulant. He or she may be called pastor, preacher, minister, leader, rector, priest, reverend, and so on. There may be other leaders in the church who help keep the church going. But, this leader is the major stimulant.

Let's use diagrams to illustrate:

Staff Member | Church Community

A

A	C	L	A
H	B	K	A
G	A	C	D
A	K	L	A

So long as the community has a larger number of (A)-types, this one staff member will create some growth possibilities. But what about all the non-A-types who are separated from the staff member by communication, language, cultural and traditional gaps? Who reaches them?

And what happens if the situation looks like this diagram?

Staff Member | Church Community

A

M	B	C	F	M
D	A	M	L	M
M	C	H	M	A
H	M	A	C	M

It appears the A-type ought to leave to make way for an M-type. Why not another alternative? Find an M-type and let him join the staff in some position the M-type recognizes as a leadership role.

No one man can be effective in all areas of the church leader functions. Once his gifts from God, natural talents and personal interests are discovered, it is time to consider expanding the staff to fill in the ministry gaps. There will be some.

Some strategists promote the fact that no one man can effectively minister to more than 110 members. Others say new staff members should be added for every 250 members. Still others feel about 350 is the time for staff expansion.

One helpful way to determine this is to diagnose the community in which the church is located. Match staff to community needs. People select churches on the basis of where their needs are met. The more variety in staff leadership the more potential variety of response.

For instance, if a community diagnosis reveals 16 percent of the population is single or divorced, should there be a person who ministers to this group? If 28 percent of the population is over sixty-five years of age, is this a potential responsibility for someone? If the divorce rate in the community is at 40 percent, is there a need for a person to focus on this situation?

Not all these staff members would require being paid a full-time salary. Some would require a stipend. Many should be lay persons whose gifts are shared with the church on the basis of community need. There are thousands of under-motivated lay persons who would give time, energy, and expertise for no remuneration if they were shown how this could create a climate for expansion growth.

This brings us to another consideration for the possibility of expanding the staff.

Developing the Class II Leader. It would be impossible to calculate the potential for expansion growth in the church if there were a mobilization of the Class II workers. The Class II worker is the unpaid volunteer who heads out and away from the church for his or her primary ministry.

Where to find the Class II Leader. These are the persons whose gifts are such they know how to relate to the unchurched. They do their best work when they are ouside the four walls of the church. They get excited about reaching new people and they stay excited about it for long periods of time. They are motivated rather than intimidated about crossing barriers with the gospel.

Some of the best Class II leaders come from the new converts. Most of their friends are unchurched. They know the methods of communication that convey meaning to the unchurched. Their relatives are emotionally involved in this decision to choose Christianity. The enthusiasm of this new convert can create a climate of awakening in the church.

A ripe field in which to find Class II workers is in the Class I working force. These are the leaders who maintain the organization and keep it functioning from week to week. Many of these have the capacity to function in both arenas. Others could step over from Class I to Class II leadership roles with some motivation.

How to help the Class II Leader:
* *Avoid overinvolvement of the Class II worker in Class I work.*
* *Train the Class II worker to keep in touch with unchurched people.*
* Develop the natural skills of the Class II worker for reaching the unchurched.
* Have special Bible studies for Class II workers. Use curriculum materials that are outreach oriented.
* Plan social activities designed along guidelines given by Class II workers.

133

* Constantly interview Class II workers to find material and strategies that create a response among the unchurched.
* Give regular support and affirmation to the Class II leader.
* Accept irregular attendance at church activities by Class II workers.
* Provide the program and atmosphere in the church that will minister to those reached through the ministry of the Class II worker.

In some instances the strategy for expanding a church staff is through fully paid personnel. Other times a small remuneration can bring a person on the staff. Many volunteers are waiting to be called upon. Any or all of these strategies are avenues for expanding the staff of a church.

The law of stimulus and response is as absolute as the law of gravity. The more personality varieties in leadership roles of the church, the more variety of response. The more specialized functions in the church, the more people with those special needs will respond. The larger number of people investing time, energy, and talent focused on reaching unchurched people, the larger number of unchurched people are reached.

Expansion growth in the church will call for expanding the staff.

There is a large field of new staff members available to most churches. So, don't remain a "one staff" church when there are some other possibilities.

Expansion Growth Brings Inconveniences

Inconveniences related to new persons.—There is no growth without inconvenience. There is no plan nor strategy that can anticipate every circumstance that growing will produce. Growth can bring in people who are not "adapted" to regular church forms and practices. Expansion growth efforts may bring in people who are not concerned with cleanliness. These people may mark on walls, misuse furniture, abuse hymn books, and disrupt the worship services by talking or moving about.

Inconveniences related to church services.—Expansion growth may cause the church to offer more than two services on Sunday. It may produce growth that extends beyond the capacity of present buildings. Spiritual learning may have to take under less than ideal conditions. Worship services may require temporary locations for long periods of time.

Inconveniences related to finances.—Expansion growth may place extreme pressures on the finances of the church. Many of those unreached people will not contribute to the financial program of the church. Young converts to Christianity often are slow to grow in their concepts of sharing the financial burden of the church. Many of them will be overobligated and time is required for them to rearrange their financial priorities.

Inconveniences of criticism.—People inside the church family may resent expansion growth. They may infer the new people get all the attention. They may assert the church needs more spiritual depth in the strategy for growth. Often complaints come because of financial burdens. The pastor will be described as being "after members only."

Leaders in other churches will join the chorus of criticism. Expansion growth is not designed to focus on church members in other churches. But, if a family or two from another church is reached problems will arise.

Denominational workers at times will tend to look with some degree of suspicion on a rapidly growing church. Subtle remarks may come forth that indicate this suspicion.

Unchurched people also have a tendency to be critical of growing churches. The financial wealth of the pastor will usually be a topic that is discussed. Or the reverse of this conversation if he is late paying his bills. Some well-meaning worker may have offended an unchurched person and he will spread the word in his sphere of influence.

Inconvenience of disruption.—Disruption means to disturb or interrupt the orderly course of affairs. Growth can produce this in a church.

* A church can lose some members if it grows too fast.
* A church can have parking problems if it grows too fast.
* A church can be forced to change many routine affairs if it grows too fast.
* A church can be required to alter service times when it grows too fast.
* The pastor may find his schedule overloaded if a church grows too fast.
* Church choirs may have "non-singers" who want to join if the church grows too fast.
* The use of new talent reached by expansion growth may introduce new methods of worship and celebration to the church.

It takes courage and determination to go on to expansion growth. The plan and strategy used cannot guarantee completely the outcome of growth. The church that decides to get outside the four walls to find growth potential must face the reality of inconvenience.

Expansion Growth Brings Change

Sidney Harris once wrote, "The liberty most men clamor for is merely the right to remain enslaved to the prejudices they have grown comfortable with." [5] Many church leaders have aspirations to be free to really change for "nongrowth" pattern, or a holding pattern to "growth" pattern. But change must be faced realistically as a definite part of the growth process.

The Menninger staff in Topeka, Kansas has noted, "All of us on the staff (900) are convinced that *all* change is experienced by *all* people as a loss and is followed by anger." [6]

Some churches can grow without a radical change. Others, obviously must undergo radical changes. The following diagram will illustrate.

```
15 ** (6) 0.8%

20 ********** (45) 5.7%

25 ************** (66) 8.3%

30 **************************** (127) 16%

35 *************************************** (164) 20.7%

40 ************************************************* (203) 25.6%

45 ***************************** (122) 15.4%

50 ********** (45) 5.7%

55 **** (13) 1.6%

60 * (1) 0.1%

65 * (1) 0.1%
```

* The factor number to the left is to indicate the ranking the churches had on a scale of 0 to 80.
* The factor number is based on four items of impact:
  1. Total church membership
  2. Total Sunday School enrollment

3. Total received by church membership by baptism
4. Total additions to the church
* A church (zzzz) with a factor total of 15 is growing at the slowest measureable growth before the actual death of the church.
* A church (ho hum) with a factor total of 40 is neither gaining nor losing members. It is holding its own.
* A church (wow) with a factor total of 65 is growing at the fastest measureable rate.

Now let's take this diagram and see how much change is required by some of these churches.

* Church (zzzzz) with a factor total of 15 cannot possibly grow without a radical change in strategy. In fact, for this church to grow it must first reach the plateau of a holding pattern. Then it must launch into growth.

* Church (ho hum) with a factor total of 40 must make some serious decisions about change if it wants to grow. But the change in strategy for this church need not be nearly so radical as for church (zzzz). But, if this church wants to move from factor total 40 to factor total 65, some radical changes will be necessary.

* Church (wow) with a factor total of 65 must be feeling good. To maintain this growth profile requires constant awareness of how to keep the church growing. Needed changes in this strategy are not usually significant because change is a way of life for them. However, if this church wants to accelerate its growth, some changes beyond their ordinary strategy will be necessary.

This diagram illustrates the growth pattern for a denomination in one state. There are 793 churches involved in this study. Of these churches 611 are in a holding pattern (factor 40), or below. These 611 churches represent approximately 77 percent of the churches in the study. Obviously, some significant changes need to occur in order for this denomination to change its growth profile in this particular state.

Change Is a Way of Life

The question is never, will we ever change? The question is: when and how much will we change? Nothing stays the same except the fact that change is always present. Churches may resist change until they ultimately go out of existence. This is a form of change. Since we must face up to and live with change, why not use it as a strategy rather than view it as a threat.

Expansion growth results leave churches no alternative. They must change or expansion growth will cease or its results be lost, or both.

Expansion growth calls for spirit-filled dreams and visions.
"I will pour out my Spirit upon all of you! Your sons and daughters will prophesy; your old men will dream dreams, and your young men see visions" (Joel 2:28, TLB). We have been so busy with the other texts concerning the coming of the Holy Spirit, that we neglect to consider this one. It is the one which most nearly corresponds to our consideration of the people of God as having a unique destiny. The destiny is to be a part of God's plan for all of history.

There is a place for the young and the old. The people of God need to be aroused to the realization that dreaming great dreams and sensing great visions of God's plans are a part of belonging to his family just as doing deeds.

What can God do in and through his chosen people? He said he could bless the whole world with them (Gen. 12). Since God kept all his promises concerning the coming of the Spirit, as he has kept all others of his promises, will he not also keep the promise that the people of God will have the capacity to dream dreams and see visions that are not available to those outside the family of God?

Concepts that must grow from spiritual dreams and visions.—Spiritual dreams and visions can create positive thinking and attitudes. A positive mental attitude is not the property of the twentieth century. A positive mental attitude comes from Christian thinking. Churches must move from negative and defensive stances. A defensive strategy leads to large portions of time being spent on protecting what we have. It fails to emphasize sharing it. Expansion growth in the church comes about through sharing those things which meet human needs.

The people of God are to be pioneers. They are meant to be adventurers. We are not settlers defending our plots of ground. We are adventurous pioneers staking out claims based on the hopes and dreams for the things which God is going to do through us.

God's people are to be seekers. We are spiritual nomads, moving at the call of God to possess new lands and win new people for the Kingdom. Our people are often mobile. The scattering of the people of God can be a positive method for scattering the good news of the gospel.

The people of God have frequently been a cultural minority. So, we must attempt tasks that will necessitate the involvement of God to accomplish. Often a struggle for spiritual survival has produced revolutionary strategies. These have experienced phenomenal proportions of success.

The church will need new visions about the types of churches for the future. "Psychological neighborhoods" must become a focal point of view. Some have more in common with those with whom they work than with those in the areas in which they live. They think alike because they work in similar thinking situations all week. Linear rather than rectangular or circular church fields could be a possibility. People living along a major thoroughfare, thirty miles long, may have more in common than those miles away from this thoroughfare.

Apartment house complexes require skills and models we have not yet been able to develop nationwide. Rudiger Reitz has said, "It takes from two to five years before residents are prone to respond positively to invitations from a minister to set up some kind of religious organization within the walls of a modern apartment house building." [7] A new vision of how to accomplish outreach and expansion growth in this setting will be required with current living trends of Americans.

The church that would launch and maintain growth in the last quarter of the twentieth century must develop what Donald McGavran calls, "church growth eyes." [8] Eyes that go beyond seeing church growth as it is and having visions of what can be.

Spirit-filled visions and dreams are rooted in the hearts of the people of God. They are sharpened by the awareness of the spiritual needs of the unreached. They can become realities with the proper motives and, adequate strategies.

Expansion Growth and Its Relationship to Extension Growth

A Concluding Remark About Expansion Growth Strategies. It is not possible to include an exhaustive list of expansion growth strategies. These are only a microcosm of the possibilities. The key is to find strategies that are suited to the needs of the people you are trying to reach in your community.

Expansion growth and extension growth make contributions to numerical church growth. But each makes a unique contribution. Each follows the other and yet each precedes the other. Expansion growth can create the climate for extension growth. It may even create a necessity for it. Expansion growth strategies can discover cross-cultural barriers that require the planting of a new unit to meet the need of a homogeneous group that is beyond the ability of a given church to meet. Extension growth may plant a new unit and as soon as this new unit takes some form of existence the expansion growth strategies will be necessary for numerical increase to take place. Both these strategies contribute to numerical church growth. They are clearly not identical. Any church that would make a serious attempt to grow by expansion must break the "stained-glass barrier" and use expansion growth strategies as the guidelines.

8
How to Turn Your Growth Curve Straight Up

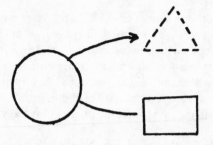

About twenty-five key leaders from First Baptist Church, Springfield, Illinois were in retreat. Several weeks of research on the growth history of their church over the last ten years had been presented. Several more hours were given to analysis, dialogue, and dreaming. The time came for the group to turn their dreams into objective, measurable goals. "What would God have us achieve in the next five years?" was the question with which the group wrestled.

Slowly, as consensus developed, the goals took form. They were immediately transferred to the large graph used to objectify the church's progress over the previous decade. A bold, dashed line was drawn from where the church stood to where the leaders wanted it to be.

Everyone sat quietly, looking at the profile. Each was silently asking, "Can we really do that much? If we can, how must we go about it?"

Someone broke into the silence. "Look at the period between 1967-71. Our growth curve at that time was almost exactly like the one we have projected for the next five years. What were we doing during that time?"

"The new church at Chatham was part of our church then," came a chorus of replies.

That was the answer, at least a large part of the answer. A village seven miles south of Springfield, already involved in suburban development, had no Baptist church. Its growing population demanded more churches. The First Baptist Church had responded to that need. During the period in question, the larger church had been involved in both *expansion* and *extension* growth.

With very few exceptions, the rate at which a church can win people from the world to faith in Christ, baptize them, and incorporate them into its fellowship will significantly increase when that church begins to meet in more than one place. Extension and bridging growth is nothing more than one church meeting in two places and evangelizing among two

143

communities of people.

Springfield Southern Baptist Church, in the same city, shows the same pattern. (See Figure 2.) This church had been in gradual decline for a decade. It continued an aggressive evangelistic program. But every time it added three new members it lost four it already had. When the church's growth history was examined, it presented a surprising picture. The percentage test revealed that in spite of the influx of new members, the church had been in decline for six of the previous ten years. (See Figure 3.)

However, right in the middle of that decline were three years of growth. What was happening those three years? Several factors, it was discovered, contributed to the growth. One was the Rochester Baptist Chapel, a daughter church in a small town east of Springfield destined for population growth.

In both these cases extension growth turned the growth curve dramatically upward.

It will do the same for your church.

Lack of Opportunity

Your response, of course, may be that there are no small, growing towns in your vicinity that are just waiting for a daughter church to be planted. That may be true. But do not accept it without careful scrutiny. We live in an age of massive mobility, shifting populations, and changing communities. All three of these are usually signs of receptivity. When communities change, even if the shift is not from one racial or language group to another, *there will be new churches.* Perhaps your church should become involved in that kind of extension or bridging growth.

Further, there are growing thousands of people in America who identify themselves as part of an ethnic community. They have the right to hear the gospel in their own heart language among their peers and to express their obedience to Christ in their own culture.

Bridging growth takes the cultural and social diversity of American life seriously. We have learned in this generation that everyone in the American "melting pot" didn't melt.[1] Nor do they want to! In fact, the "melting pot" scenario has always been a myth. Most of those who were part of the predominate culture, Caucasian and English-speaking, resisted vigorously the efforts of blacks, American Indians, and Mexican-Americans to assimilate.

Now America is a varied and colorful mosaic of race, culture, and national origin.[2] One out of ten Americans are black and one out of twenty have a Spanish surname. One-half million speak an American Indian language in their homes. Another half million prefer Japanese to English. Still another half million have another Asian tongue as their heart language. Nor does it stop there. A New England Yankee and a Southerner may both speak English, but they often have trouble understanding each other and even greater difficulty understanding each others "ways."

There are thousands of communities, cultural and geographic, that require that we both make new disciples and begin daughter churches. Commitment to these ministries will accelerate the growth rate of the mother church and is essential obedience to the Great Commission of Jesus Christ.

Enough Is Enough

If extension and bridging growth are so effective, why have so few churches been involved? We believe there are several reasons.

1. For most of this century, and especially during the last two decades, many Christian leaders have played down the need for new churches. In an age that has emphasized social action and ecumenical interests, the romance has been with church mergers, not church planting, and with the application of the gospel to various issues and systems of society, not the gathering of churches in the various segments of society.

2. Many Christians, who do not see the diversity that is American society, or who insist that cultural diversity must be ignored or overcome through evangelism, insist that we already have too many churches. Enough is enough!

3. Superior roadways and rapid transportation—both private and public—have made established meeting houses accessible to people from distant communities.

4. Our struggle to overcome social, cultural, and racial segregation within churches has idealized conglomerate churches and mitigated against starting churches in the various segments of society.

5. The prevalent infatuation with "giant" churches—from whatever motivation—has caused many church leaders to resist the planting of new churches as a threat to empire.

6. Ecclesiastical *detente* among American Christians in this century has produced something of a religious settlement among the various denominations, and it has become unthinkable if Southern Baptists, for example, consider beginning a daughter church where there are no "Southern Baptist prospects." Everyone, this mentality suggests, has some "preference." To attempt to win a person to active allegiance to Christ and add

him to a congregation different from his "preference" is unabashedly called "proselyting."

How to Have a Baby

How can a church become involved in extension or bridging growth?

In reality, those things required for bringing "baby" churches into the world are similar to those required for prospective parents. We will discuss some of the basic principles of *ecclesiastical obstetrics* and *pediatrics*.[3]

I

Ecclesiastical Obstetrics

Three principles should be followed in the process of bringing a daughter church to birth.[4]

Principle One: Parenthood should be planned.

Extension and, to a lesser degree, bridging growth have often been unplanned. Efforts of this kind have sometimes been disorganized, ill-conceived, improperly motivated, and more an expression of hostility between brothers than of obedience to God.

This need not be true in your church. A sure way to ensure that it does not take place is to develop a total strategy for church growth which includes all growth dimensions. In this total strategy there must be a church planting strategy. In short, churches should practice planned parenthood.

At least three steps are needed to guarantee planned church planting.

1. Get the church organized for extension and bridging growth. Steps can be taken to develop a congregational structure for beginning daughter churches. Here are five suggestions.

a. *Assign leadership to responsible lay persons.* Select a Church Missions Committee (CMC) within the congregation. Put the responsibility for this significant function of the church on the shoulders of lay leaders. It is tragic—but true—that, since 1886, Matthew 28:19–20 in the minds of most American Christians has been the exclusive domain of the overseas mission. This has given a distorted view of the mission of the church to the average church member. By making missions the sole responsibility of those specially called and trained for cross-cultural evangelism and of national and regional boards and societies, usually in distant cities, it has robbed the church as a whole of the glory of direct involvement in the most primary of all mission tasks—that of gathering new disciples of Christ into new, growing congregations.

This action will also counteract a most unscriptural notion that is abroad today, that responsibility for starting new churches in the American context belongs to state, regional, and national boards or societies and is divorced from the essential duties of churches or individuals.

b. *Give the CMC status in the congregation.* It should rank along with the Church Council, Board of Christian Education, the Budget and Finance Committee, the Youth Council, and so on, as a primary agent in the administration of the total ministry of the church.

c. *Choose members for the CMC who provide creative, forceful leadership.* It is so easily, and often, done another way. All other leadership positions in the church organizations are filled, and those structured with responsibility beyond the immediate community of the church are manned by the unwilling and/or inept. These persons should have a missionary and evangelical passion and a personal faith that is contagious. They should be able and willing to devote time to gathering and analyzing data about community needs. They should command the attention and respect of the congregation when they speak.

d. *Train the CMC for its job.* Begin with bare essentials. Do *not* share all the minute details at a one-and-only training session. Let the CMC begin to function, and then provide continual training opportunities that are dictated by functional needs. This approach vastly increases the relevancy to training information and provides high motivation for training opportunities.[5]

e. *Turn the CMC loose to function.* There are at least five primary functions of a CMC:

1) *A prophetic function.* Churches have, since the Jerusalem Church of Acts, tended to become ingrown, exclusive, self-centered, and institutionalized. The CMC, by calling the church back to the biblical mandate and by sharing the needs of communities, must become the Jiminy Cricket of its modern ecclesiastical Pinocchio.

2) *A planning function.* The CMC must develop church growth eyes just as a student pilot must develop navigation eyes. It must be able to recognize evidence of unreached pockets of people. This function is not primarily intuitive. It requires study of census data and housing and economic patterns. Recognition is only the beginning. The CMC must develop strategies to penetrate unreached populations and gather new congregations. The

147

strategies must be communicated to the congregation.

3) *A promotion function.* The findings and recommendations of the CMC should be publicized, reported, discussed, and gossiped throughout the entire membership. Do not restrict the reports to the meetings of the congregation. Both need and potential should be emphasized. The CMC should make a church planting project as exciting and pervasive as an every-member financial canvass, an evangelistic campaign, or a building program.

4) *An enlistment function.* Churches have within their membership individuals and families who have particular gifts for getting new churches started. The CMC should in every way possible attempt to discover people with those gifts and interests. They should share the church planting needs and their plans with the congregation in such a way as to evoke such gifts that might be latent in individuals.

5) *An implementation function.* The CMC must have authority, resources, an initiative to see that plans are carried out, evaluated, and reshaped until they prove effective.

By these or other similar steps, an organizational structure can be formalized within a congregation with responsibility for undertaking extension or bridging growth.

2. Cooperate with the missions committee or committee for new church development of your local association, conference, or synod. This step is extremely important if such a group exists and actually functions. It will provide for more pervasive cooperation, will limit the danger of misunderstanding between sister churches, and will save from duplicating expenditures in man-hours and money.

This group will have an area strategy for new churches and, because of research already done, can be of invaluable assistance in performing the next step in planned parenthood for a church.[6]

3. Select the general geographical area and the specific target people on the basis of hard research. Do away with guesswork. Don't be duped by the availability of an abandoned building. Acquiring an old church building is often one of the most detrimental things that can be done for a beginning congregation. First, let the Holy Spirit create the new community, then the new community can acquire the kind of building they can use and provide for financially.

We do not suggest that the leadership of the Holy Spirit is not required or that prayer has no place in the choice of a location for a daughter church. Nor do we suggest that it is *never* right to acquire a building before some semblance of a congregation is gathered. We are suggesting that the Holy Spirit can and does lead us as we give careful attention to the cultural, racial, economic, and geographic communities that are around us. We do insist that new churches should be started where there are communities of people who need to be introduced to Jesus Christ, not where church-type facilities happen to be for rent or sale. Daughter churches can begin in homes, banks, schools, firehouses, motel rooms, and many other good places. Private facilities should be provided only when it becomes absolutely necessary.

Principle Two: Make practical preparations for parenthood.

When we speak of planned parenthood for churches, we speak of deliberate plans to grow through extension and bridging patterns. Other preparations must be made. Just as an expectant mother prepares herself physically, mentally, and psychologically for the birth of a child, preparation should be made to get the church ready to become a mother. Attention also needs to be given to the community about to receive the new congregation. Is it prepared, receptive, and aware of what is about to take place? We suggest three kinds of preparation for the church expecting soon to become a mother.

1. Lay a spiritual foundation in the congregation for starting a daughter church.

What steps can be taken to develop a passion for this kind of church growth? We will suggest five.

a. *Set church planting in biblical perspective.* The mission of the church succinctly, if simplistically stated, is to proclaim the gospel of Jesus Christ in the power of the Holy Spirit among all the social groupings of mankind, and to gather those who hear into churches. Planting churches is right at the heart of the apostolate of the church of the New Testament. Planting churches is the essence of the apostolic gift. Evangelism (winning to commitment to Christ) is not complete until churches are gathered. In preaching and teaching, the importance and centrality of church planting needs to be embedded in the congregation.

b. *Magnify the ministry of the laity.* The responsibility for beginning a daughter church should never be conceived as the labor of the clergy. Adequate spiritual preparation should include a clear concept of the significance of the ministry of all the people of God. Men and women are called to meaningful spiritual ministry, not just to menial "secular" tasks. Biblically and historically it has been the laity mobilized and motivated to spiritual ministry that has produced the spontaneous expansion of the church.

149

c. *Maximize the central place of the Holy Spirit in the mission of the church, and emphasize the necessity and possibility for every believer to be filled and led by the Spirit of God.* The Spirit of God is the spirit of growing churches. He is the executor of God's mission to the world in Christ. The purpose of God in redemption, the plan of God for the ages, is to be actualized by the ministry of the Spirit working in and through the church.

Everyone agrees on the central place of the Spirit in church growth. Personal, experiential acquaintance with the Holy Spirit's work in the individual Christian life has been harder to come by since the rise of Pentecostalism during the first decade of this century. Nevertheless, adequate spiritual preparation for extension and bridging growth in a local congregation demands that we teach:

1) the necessity for all believers to be filled with and walk in the Spirit.

2) the need for all Christians to be led by the Spirit in daily lives and to surrender themselves to God as instruments of righteousness, and then become productive members of the body of Christ.

3) the responsibility of believers to attempt to discover the particular gift given by the Spirit, and to exercise it so that the church might be built up and continue to grow.

4) that the Holy Spirit empowers the most backward Christian for effective ministry and witness.[7]

d. *Provide opportunity for periodic renewal.* The need to recreate must be met if a church is to maintain the spiritual dynamic essential to church planting. The body of Christ must be built up, as well as added to. Edification and evangelism are the twin tasks that constantly face the church. Retreats, or small groups for Bible study and prayer groups are two ways to pursue this step.

e. *Make evangelism the life-style of the church.* A church which regularly wins men and women to Christ from the world can begin a daughter church which will do the same. Effective and habitual efforts in direct evangelism will also contribute to the spiritual foundation most essential to getting a church ready for church planting.[8]

2. Develop a mentality in the congregation for beginning a new church.

What steps can be taken to create a mental climate for church planting? Several matters deserve attention.

a. *Actualize mission philosophy.* It is amazing how many missionary churches are not missionary. They may have a stated theory of missionary concern and have a limited commitment to the financial support of overseas missions, but never consider actualizing their missionary philosophy by direct support and personal involvement. The missionary nature of the congregation is only a rumor. One way a CMC can prepare the sponsoring church for church planting is to specify the mission philosophy of the church—first in words, and then in concrete challenges. They should focus on real opportunities for the church membership to practice what is preached in missionary terms.

b. *Be realistic about social, cultural, and geographical boundaries.* A congregation—no matter how large—which meets in Hammond, Indiana, cannot adequately minister to Waukegan, Illinois, over fifty miles away, no matter how large the bus or how dedicated the workers. As obvious as that may be, there are hundreds of churches which are presently attempting that strategy. Most of them do not do it as effectively as the church in Hammond.

Cultural and social boundaries are just as real as geographical boundaries. There are conglomerate churches, composed of groupings from various socioeconomic, racial, and cultural strata, but these are few, and the men who can lead them are rare. Most of us share our most effective witness within certain related pieces of the human mosaic. We do not communicate effectively across significant cultural lines.

Underline the facts that men do not like to cross cultural and social barriers to become Christians, that we most readily and effectively witness to our peers, and that churches grow along these larger family lines. This needs to be recognized as reality, so that the mother church can see the need for planting daughter churches in every segment of human society. It is patently unchristian to insist that the only way a garbage man can become a Christian and an active church member is in the church where vice-presidents of the banks are principal leaders.

c. *Combat local church myopia.* There is an innate shortsightedness in mankind, a tendency to look at the local, at what is ours, and to focus full energies in that direction. One's own community, no matter how needy, is not the world. Congregations develop something akin to militant nationalism in reference to their own church. It seems rational to say, "Why should we preach the gospel in other places when we have not won our own community as yet?" Such a philosophy would have confined Christianity to Judea and Galilee, an insignificant sect of Judaism.

d. *Be honest about small church efficiency.* We are living in a "big" church era. Church and church staff size have become a status symbol. But, the truth is that small churches are much more efficient in terms of

151

evangelism than large churches. Southern Baptists can provide us with an illustration. In 1972, SBC churches between 2,000 and 3,000 in membership averaged sixty-eight baptisms. That same year the churches with membership 200-300 averaged ten baptisms. Ten smaller churches (200-300) would have baptized thirty-two more people than one large church (2,000-3,000).

This requires mental toughness in a day of big church romance. This information needs to be shared with the budding mother church.[9]

e. *Cultivate the spirit of achievement.* A positive mental attitude is essential to constant achievement. The church is called to victory, to growth, and to the multiplication of units. A church which believes that under God it can, can! One of the most essential factors to proper mental preparation for church planting is a spirit of faith, victory, and confidence permeating the congregation and its leaders. A church that expects great things from God can attempt great things for God.

3. Condition the community for the new church. The soil must be prepared for planting. Cultivation must take place to ensure, as far as possible, that the congregation will be planted in a climate of receptivity rather than hostility. There are situations where hostility from some segments of a community is inevitable. This was true for first-century Christians as well. Don't be dismayed if it happens. Do everything possible to see that it does not, short of being disobedient to God.

Three suggestions may serve as guidelines in discovering methods of soil preparation.

a. *Survey the community.* Find out where the unchurched people live and what their names are.[10] In the process you will also discover those unenlisted, inactive Christians who live there. This may be done by telephone or house-to-house. The latter is by far the most effective and most conducive to helpful cultivation. By careful training of workers it is also possible in this survey to discover the felt-needs in the community. This is essential to discover those ministries that should characterize the new congregation. A "cup of cold water" given in Christ's name assumes a person who is thirsty. If there is no thirst, there is no ministry, only arrogance.

b. *Personal get-acquainted visits should follow up the survey.* Perhaps a letter of appreciation to those who were especially responsive and helpful would be wise. A series of cultivative letters can be used with those who are unchurched and unenlisted. A program of cultivative visitation should precede the actual birth of the new congregation. A community-wide Scripture distribution plan is often effective. It usually creates a warm atmosphere of appreciation and opens up doors to responsive people. The point is that deliberate efforts should be made to make as many friends as possible and collect the names of as many unchurched people as possible before the new congregation begins to meet.

c. *Condition the community through the ministry of groups.* Youth choirs, for example, are often very effective in the cultivation process. They can give concerts in public places, conduct Backyard Bible Clubs, carry on day camps, create public park ministries, and assist in a variety of ways that will prepare the community for the new church. Many other groups can do the same. All means possible should be used to present an attractive witness to Jesus Christ, to create responsiveness in the community, and to make friends for the daughter church even before it begins.

Principle Three: Bring the new church to birth with expectancy, vigor, and joy.

How does a church approach the day that extension or bridging growth begins? Attitude is the magic word. A mother-to-be can condition herself physically for the birth of a new child. It is equally important to condition herself mentally. The same thing is true for a budding mother church.

1. *Set a day to begin.* It's an exciting day in a home when a family learns when the new baby is going to arrive. Though this excitement may be mixed with some anxiety and a little trepidation. But nothing really tops it—except the actual day of arrival. The same principles are at work when the church sets the day for beginning a daughter church. Determining the birthday makes the project take on reality. It tends to telescope planning and preparation, and it generates excitement, anticipation, prayer, and personal commitment.

If there is no target date, assignments can be delayed and the actual beginning can be postponed indefinitely. In a family a new baby's arrival, once it has been determined the baby is coming, is almost inevitable! At least it can't be forever postponed. However, it does not work that way for churches. Hundreds of churches have planned to start daughter churches, but never get around to it. One reason is that they did not have a definite day to begin.

Setting a day is important for another reason. "Beginning," a proverb says, "is half done." That proverb is true. It is amazing how easily most things go once they get started. So, set a day!

Perhaps here we should answer the question, How do new churches begin? Are there different ways a new church can be born?

Yes. There are several different methods for getting a daughter church underway. Many churches are born out of *unhappy* divisions. This is one problem we are attempting to meet by insisting on planned parenthood for churches. Then new churches are viewed as a strategy for the growth of the church not a plan for the splintering of the church. However, there are many daughter churches that are born from *happy* divisions. A church asks a fairly large group from its fellowship to begin meeting in another geographical area. New churches are born through both these procedures.

Neither of these two patterns are the norm. Usually, a daughter church is planted in another geographic or cultural community with very few leaders from the mother church and designed to reach the unchurched and unenlisted in that community. Even these, however, may come into existence through various methods.

There are four different methodological categories for beginning daughter churches:[11]

a. *Bible study and/or prayer groups in the community.* In fact, one rule to follow when going into a new community where you have no contacts is to look for a group that is praying. This was the method of Paul and Silas in Philippi. People who are searching the Bible and seeking for reality are responsive to the message of Christ. Out of the "Riverside Prayer Group" in Philippi came the "Church of Joy" that was so helpful in Paul's later ministry.

A home opened up to Bible study and unsaved friends invited to participate soon leads to conversions to Christ and the spiritual *koinonia* essential to a church. This fellowship stage for the daughter church is usually essential to stability in the daughter church.

b. *Group worship experience.* Sometimes, through a survey, enough interested people can be found to begin regular Sunday worship services at once. This is not often true nor is it always the best procedure. It is sometimes detrimental to move too quickly to this kind of ministry without giving opportunity for the Holy Spirit to really create community through a fellowship period. But thousands of daughter churches have begun just this way. Some men are especially gifted at church planting and seem to be able to begin at this level. More often, if new churches are led by laymen, a fellowship period is required.

c. *Evangelistic events and organizations.* Hundreds of new churches have been started as a result of a concentrated evangelistic effort in a community. In most cases several days of evangelistic services, supported by prayer and door-to-door visitation, has been the method. However, some churches have begun with nothing more than a Vacation Bible School that resulted in the conversion of several children who proved to be bridges to their families and others. Sunday Schools have been very excellent methods for planting daughter churches. New Sunday Schools, conducted on Sunday afternoons, evenings, or other times, often eventually become daughter churches.

d. *Community ministries.* Some daughter churches have been started as a result of a direct service ministry in a community. Usually, these are not originally planned to produce new churches but to meet obvious social needs. In the process of meeting needs and bearing witness to Jesus Christ, people have been persuaded to believe in Jesus, follow him in baptism, and become the nucleus of a new congregation.

2. *Make the birthday a day of joy.* Celebration should mark the birthday of a daughter church. It is a day for rejoicing.

There are several things that can be done to guarantee that it will be a joyous time. All modern books for expectant parents have taken up Dr. Grantly Dick-Read's emphasis, in *Childbirth Without Fear,* on a positive mental attitude toward the birth process. Childbirth, we are learning, need not be an unbearable experience, but is a simple, joyful, and natural act. Extension and bridging growth, the process of multiplying congregation, likewise is not unbearable, but a simple, joyful, and natural function for a church. It is one of the marks of a living organism. Approaching it in that way is the first key to making the birthday of a daughter church a wonderful occasion.

Secondly, get as many people involved in the process as possible from the mother church. Many obstetricians maintain that the birth of a child was not only intended to be a soul-inspiring act of cooperation in conception but also in delivery. Fathers are trained to share in the birth event. The entire church should be mobilized in prayer support for the beginning of a new fellowship or chapel. Have as many people as possible participating in the detailed activities necessary to get the daughter church underway. Reports of both victories and problems need to be shared with the full membership of the mother church as often and early as possible.

Finally, since celebration is a characteristic of the people of God in both Old and New Testaments, make the birthday of the daugher church a grand church occasion. You don't have to give away cigars, but do something that will say to the full membership and to the community that an extraordinarily important event has taken place.

3. *Give it all you've got!* The birth process is a combination of relaxation and labor. Prenatal training always includes careful instructions in the art of relaxation as well as the sharing of factual information and

muscle toning. Getting a new congregation underway is much the same. It demands trust in God and determined efforts to be faithful to him in evangelism and witness. Successful church planters have learned how to balance those two.

It is easy to become hesitant, negative, and timid when a daughter church is about to begin. After all, the ministry is probably small, in a community of people with whom the church is not well acquainted, and takes place at some distance from the building of the mother church. To succumb this kind of rationale is a great mistake. For a pastor the most lasting and significant combination he can make during a pastorate could well be the daughter churches he helps to plant. Long after his ministry has been forgotten at the mother church those new churches will continue to make disciples and plant other churches. For many lay persons, the catalyst that set them on the road to Christian maturity and effectiveness will be their involvement in a beginning congregation. The importance of what is being done demands best efforts.

For a church or individual to "give it all they've got" is the best guarantee of success. Most churches, and individuals, fail not because of lack of talent or resources, but because they do not give their best. This is especially true with beginning daughter churches.

II

Ecclesiastical Pediatrics

After the new church has begun, what can be done to assure wholesome and constant growth? Here are five simple rules for *ecclesiastical pediatrics*.

Rule One: Be sure the "baby" church has proper feeding.

More new congregations die from spiritual malnutrition than any other cause. Improper and inadequate diet opens the doors for many other problems. The primary reason for doctrinal instability, evangelistic ineffectiveness, and spiritual disunity in new congregations is dull, uninspired, impractical Bible teaching.

New Christians and those Christians reclaimed from inactivity usually have no scriptural foundation on which to build their new life in Christ. They do not need all the academic detail that characterizes much modern Bible teaching material. They need to have the Bible inform their view of themselves and the world around them. They need a biblical world view to give order and direction to their lives. They feel need for very pragmatic applications of biblical truth to the problems that plague their lives. This can only come by a practical yet systematic approach to Bible teaching.

We have a strong conviction that Sunday morning Bible teaching programs alone are usually unable to meet this need. What is done on Sunday morning needs to be supplemented with much more in-depth, relational exposure to the Bible. Subjects that should be covered in a course on the biblical foundations for mature Christian living should include the following:

(1) The Greatest Man Who Ever Lived: An Introduction to the Life of Jesus
(2) Life's Greatest Adventure: Your Life in the Son
(3) Life's Greatest Adventure: The Son in Your Life
(4) The Christian and the Holy Spirit
(5) The Christian and Prayer
(6) The Christian and the Bible
(7) The Christian Witness
(8) The Christian and Stewardship
(9) The Christian and Spiritual Gifts
(10) The Christian and Obedience
(11) The Christian Home
(12) The Christian and the Church

Rule Two: Be sure the "baby" church gets love, acceptance, and support.

Pediatricians and child psychologists insist that the love and affection, the care and tenderness, that a new baby receives in the first few months of his life have a tremendous effect on the emotional development of the person for the rest of his life. In reference to daughter churches this means, do not birth it and drop it! Take steps to secure concrete involvement of the mother church in the life of the daughter church. There needs to be *continuing commitment* from the mother church. At least four areas demand attention.

1. *Commitment in terms of prayer.* Continue to undergird the project with prayer. Prayer must not be viewed as exotic and mystical, but essential and pragmatic. Prayer is not penultimate or, even, antepenultimate to the ministry of the church. It is the place to begin, continue, and end any ministry of witness or service in the name of Jesus. Specific plans should be made, and individuals and organizations in the church should be enlisted for concerted, sustained, and explicit prayer support for the

daughter church.

Practically speaking, the first concrete commitment of the church should be in a program of persistent and fervent prayer.

2. *Commitment in terms of training.* Equip the congregation with the skills necessary for gathering new churches. Church training programs—except for some devised in very recent years—have been basically maintenance oriented. We have produced a host of workers who know how to conduct a business meeting and are acquainted with the latest in educational psychology. We have produced very few who make personal witnessing a way of life, who are always touching others with Christ.

Provide training for many outreach strategies. Most outreach training has been in only two areas: personal evangelism and bus ministry. We need to provide training for other options. Bible clubs and community ministries are examples.

This practical training must be tied directly to spiritual preparation. It is impossible to share life-at-its-best if you are not experiencing life-at-its-best. The two must go hand in hand.

Pragmatically, new churches demand *relevant* training opportunities.

3. *Commitment in terms of money.* Underwrite the project with *necessary* funding. We do not speak here of total support. Some churches have refused to sponsor daughter churches because they could not buy a site, erect a first unit, and put a full-time seminary graduate on the field. Other churches will sponsor a daughter church *only* if it requires *no* support with money or people. To both these extremes we call for commitment of *necessary* funding.

In funding, priorities need to be established. People are much more important than places. Many new churches have been aborted because no "worthy" meeting place could be found for rent or because no place could be found to build a building. The best money will be spent in personnel. Halls should be rented only when homes are unavailable or too small. Buildings should be erected as a last resort.

Pragmatically, new churches demand financial commitment just as other programs demand monetary resources.

4. *Commitment in terms of people.* Ask the church to commit people—individuals and families—to daughter churches just as it commits people to Bible study organizations, to organizations for missionary education and music, or to social activism.

Many new churches have begun with sponsorship in name only. No people and no dollars were committed. This chapter is a plea to move away from that kind of mothering. It is so much better when a church will invest part of its life in the daughter church by providing at least part of the nucleus in the new community.

The New Testament pattern in evangelism is not to make new disciples and leave them unrelated to other Christians. Neither is the biblical pattern to enlarge existing churches until their membership numbers in the thousands. The biblical pattern is to move converts into new churches, let them meet in homes, and multiply the number of such churches. We believe this is a healthy pattern for today. "Normal growth comes by the division of cells, not by the unlimited expansion of existing cells. The growth of individual cells beyond a certain point is pathological." [12]

The only way to increase the ratio of Christians to population in any nation is to multiply the number of churches. If Evangelicals are to make a significant contribution to bringing America to Christ, the number of churches must be multiplied.

Finally, there can be continued commitment of personnel on other than a permanent or semipermanent basis. Groups of men, women, and young people can be enlisted for community events and ministries, for surveys, special projects, and evangelistic campaigns. Involvement of the whole church in the project over several years is very desirable.

Pragmatically, new churches demand the involvement of people in services and witness.

Rule Three: Don't expect instant maturity.

Very few daughter churches have been started without problems! Problems should be expected.

Young churches very often have problems like young children. Many of them can be predicted. To anticipate them is the first step toward their solution.

Many of the problems that develop in a daughter church are problems of relationship with the mother church. These can usually be avoided if relationships are spelled out clearly. At least four problem areas seem to occur over and over again.[13]

1. *How are members to be received?* Since the daughter church is an extension of the mother church in another community, members should be received according to the policy of the mother church. The mother church should maintain a separate roll for daughter's church members since it will eventually become a separate church.

2. *How is the pastor called?* Lay leadership will probably characterize the early days of the daughter church. Eventually, however, both mother and daughter will recognize the need for a pastor for daughter church. Guidelines for this would be determined by the church polity of the

congregation. It should be clearly understood. In churches with congregational polity, the call should be issued concurrently, but officially through the mother church.

3. *How is business to be conducted?* Again church polity will determine policy. It should be clearly spelled out to the daughter church as to the extent of its authority. If at all possible, there should be official representatives from the mother church at congregational meeting of daughter church and vice versa. Actions taken by daughter church should be carefully related to the mother church.

4. *How are finances to be managed?* It is probably best for the mother church to maintain a separate financial record of the income of the daughter church and make a complete accounting of funds to the mission. As the daughter church develops organically, it may be able to assume the management of its finances.

Other more serious problems may develop. These can be predicted and avoided. Whatever policy is developed about them should not be considered ironclad and eternal. The policies should be subject to change as the daugher church grows both numerically and organically.

Rule Four: Permit progressive, natural growth.

True organic growth cannot be pushed. It must develop naturally. Some churches wish to move the daughter church to independent status too quickly. This is most often true when the project was begun with negative mental attitudes and insufficient preparation. In this chapter we have referred to the three stages in the development of a daughter church. The time has come for us to define them. To be sure, either of the first two stages may be bypassed and a new and independent congregation can be immediately constituted. But this three stage development is normative. Each of the first two stages has its value.

1. *The fellowship period.*[14] The earliest stage in the development of a daughter church is often called the fellowship period. It is that period when small groups are used most extensively in extension and bridging growth processes.

Some feel that this period is part of the process of cultivating the community in preparation for launching the daughter church. To be sure, it is the embryonic stage before the full-blown chapel period. But we consider it the infant age of the daughter church.

Several fellowship models can be used, or a combination of any of them.[15] Usually those designed for Bible study and prayer and which maintain an evangelistic passion are most effective.

The question is, Is the fellowship necessary and what are its values?

The valuable contribution the fellowship makes to the daughter church is just what makes it necessary.

(1) The fellowship period permits the Holy Spirit to create *koinonia*. Its value is that it solidifies the group. The fellowship brings people who have not know each other together. They get to know each other. They become a body.

(2) The fellowship period makes it possible to expand the operational base for the daughter church. Several fellowships can be conducted in the same community during a given week. The daughter church will be reaching different people in several different places. Growth possibilities will be multiplied. Periodically, the various fellowships can be brought together for a time of larger fellowship and worship.

(3) The fellowship period provides a time for training leaders for the daughter church. The biblical foundation so necessary to Christian maturity can actually be started in the fellowship period. This approach is highly desirable. New Christians need to be trained immediately to share Christ with their peers. The fellowship period provides that opportunity.

(4) The fellowship period provides time to build a financial base for the daughter church. We are not suggesting at this point that every fellowship begin at once to take an offering. That may be desirable for some. As the fellowship becomes a group, the desire to give usually develops spontaneously. Consensus develops in the group about the need to move toward the chapel stage and to provide for a pastor. This is most important for building an adequate financial base.

(5) The fellowship period can set a person-centered ministry pattern for the daughter church. Small group dynamics function effectively only in the personal dimension. New churches that begin in the fellowship models tend to develop a ministry life-style that is responsive to the individual and his felt need.

(6) The fellowship period constitutes excellent preparation for the chapel period. A daughter church that grows primarily through conversion growth needs time to permit these new Christians to learn to function in public worship and corporate life. Small group experience provides this opportunity.

2. *The chapel period.* The second stage in the development of daughter churches is more formal and public than the first. It usually develops after there has been considerable numerical increase through the various fellowships. This period should follow recognizable organic growth. The inner structure of the daughter church needs to develop and leadership is needed for the first semblance of organization.

The chapel period describes that time in the life of a new church when it begins to meet for public worship, in a central place, usually on Sunday morning. This period makes some demands on the daughter church that have not been made before.

a. A permanent meeting place and regular hours for public worship are required. Bible study groups in the fellowship period may vary in place and time. This cannot continue in the chapel period. By permanent we do not, of course, mean a building exclusively owned and used by the daughter church. Rented, borrowed, or leased facilities may be adequate.

b. Equipment not usually required in the fellowship stage are demanded during this period. Hymnals, chairs, offering plates, pianos, and organs are usually necessary for public worship.

c. Lay-led organizations are usually created and become an integral part of the ministry of the daughter church in the chapel period. A Sunday School should be launched at the same time regular Sunday morning worship service is begun. This demands leadership at a level not required in the fellowship period.

d. Leaders of public worship are needed in the chapel period. Someone should be enlisted to direct the congregational singing and to deliver the sermon. An ordained, seminary trained minister is not necessarily demanded. Laymen often are eloquent and effective preachers. Nevertheless, the Word of God must be proclaimed in a manner somewhat different than in the earlier period.

It is obvious that the chapel period is necessary for the developing daughter church. It is a natural and progressive step on the way to stage three.

3. *The constituted church.* The final stage arrives when the daughter church is formally constituted into a church. This period will not be discussed at length in this chapter. It will be sufficient at this point, to suggest that there are, at least, three criteria for determining if a daughter church is ready for this stage:

a. Does the daughter church have doctrinal integrity?
b. Does it have adequate leadership to carry on its ministries and maintain its corporate life?
c. Does it have financial stability?

Rule Five: Encourage the "baby" church to walk alone.

One temptation that faces the mother church is to nudge the daughter church too quickly to separate existence as a church. But the most pervasive temptation is quite the opposite. The mother church often wants to keep the daughter church under its domain, and it discourages progress toward independent constitution. This is especially a problem for those churches engaged in bridging growth. Often overwhelming paternalism produces reluctance to grant the daughter church independent church status.

The mother church should take deliberate steps to ensure that the daughter church will not always maintain a dependent relationship. One goal to be constantly held before the two congregations is that the daughter church become truly indigenous to the community in which it is planted.

What does this involve? Traditionally, indigenous churches have been identified as those which are self-propagating, self-supporting, and self-governing. These three attributes are very important. Periodic evaluation should be made of the progress in the daughter church in this direction. Is the new congregation being successful in its own evangelism program? Is there measurable progress toward self-support? Is leadership developing so that responsible government can be developed?

However, progress in this direction is not really enough. A more important aspect of indigenousness has to do with culture. Is the new church really composed of people in the community where it is planted? This is a fundamental question. The mother church should assess this factor with regularity. Deliberate efforts to develop leaders from the target community and to progressively turn the responsibility for the daughter church over to them is an axiom of growth by extension and bridging methods.

Postscript

Early in this chapter reference was made to two churches which were able to show significant growth through planting daughter churches in nearby municipalities. Is extension growth a real possibility in areas of stable or declining population, and is it really necessary and desirable where there is already a church that people can attend?

Consider the Elkton Baptist Church, Elkton, Kentucky, and the daughter church it planted less than two blocks from its building.

Elkton is a small county seat town in southwestern Kentucky, about sixty miles north of Nashville, Tennessee (population 1,634). Elkton Baptist Church is the largest church of any sort in all of Todd County. It is rather prestigious with businessmen, professional people, and large farm owners and operators in its membership.

In July 1962, an effort was made to reach the people in the town and county who felt uncomfortable at the "big" church. An evangelistic campaign was conducted in a tent. A number of people were converted to Christ. In spite of their new faith in Christ, they still felt ill-at-ease in the larger, more socially prestigious congregation.

On July 25, a mission chapel was opened in a remodeled storefront a short distance from the Elkton Baptist Church building. Sunday School enrollment was twenty-five. In five years, the daughter church had 132 Sunday School members. Four years later, in 1971, the Calvary Baptist Church was organized. In 1977, it had 207 resident members and over 300 enrolled in Sunday School.

The daughter church detracted not in the least from the mother church. In fact, until the new church was organized, the pastor of the mother church served as pastor of the chapel and preached there both morning and evening services. The growth of the mother church between 1966-1970 was startling. One of the reasons was that it became involved in extension growth.

This chapter has been designed to suggest ways a church can follow through to bridging and extension growth. F. J. Redford, Department of Church Extension, Home Mission Board, SBC, has developed nine steps as a guide for establishing new churches. They will provide an adequate review for this chapter.[16]

Step One:	Elect a Church Missions Committee.
Step Two:	Select the geographic area.
Step Three:	Prepare the church for outreach.
Step Four:	Cultivate the mission field.
Step Five:	Begin with mission fellowships.
Step Six:	Grow toward a mission chapel.
Step Seven:	Develop a sound financial base.
Step Eight:	Defer building plans until program makes one necessary and finances make it possible.
Step Nine:	Constitute the new church when spiritual maturity is evident.

9
Marks of Growing Churches

Churches grow in all kinds of circumstances. No particular physical situation guarantees or limits growth. *The growth your church will experience during the next five years need not be directly related to the size or condition of the building you have right now.* Some churches grow with fabulous facilities in fantastic locations within flourishing communities. Other churches grow with literally no facilities of their own, on undesirable side streets, and in impoverished communities. Still others decline and die in both situations.

Growth is not determined by the level of the academic achievement of the leadership of a church. Many churches have leaders with the best formal education their culture affords. Some of them experience a steady persistent growth; others have a growth explosion; and others quietly fade away. Some churches have leaders who not only have no formal education, but publicly belittle it. Most of those never grow, and eventually disappear. Others grow consistently and may eventually end up establishing a college or seminary!

Growth is not determined by the level of social acceptance a church may have in its community. Churches highly favored by civil leaders and their culture may grow or decline. Some churches are considered social outcasts and experience constant harassment by civil authority, but even persecution will not stop growth.

Growth is not determined by purity of doctrine. Some groups are paragons of biblical orthodoxy and move steadily toward extinction. Their explanation is, "Men have itching ears. They will not hear the *true* Word of God. It is our preaching of *the truth* without compromise that keeps us from growing." Other groups hold the same essential doctrines, preach them with the same fervor, and grow all the while. Their explanation is, "God always blesses his *true* Word when it is preached. It is the preaching of *the truth* without compromise that causes us to grow."

Growth is not solely determined by the measure of separation, the evidence of vital holiness, or the emphasis on the Holy Spirit that is found in the church. Do not misunderstand at this point. There is no "growth that is from God" except that produced by the Holy Spirit. However, it is possible to be so separated from the world that there is no vital contact with the lost men who live in that world. There can be no growth without loving, caring relationships with outsiders. People can become so enmeshed in the pursuit of holiness and exotic spiritual experience that they are no longer able to relate meaningfully with modern pagans. For this reason some churches emphasize holiness, separation, and total dependence on the Holy Spirit, and never grow. Other churches have the same emphasis, and articulate about it with excitement, and grow spontaneously.

Do growing churches have other things in common besides growth? Are there any distinctive marks of growing churches? Are there common denominators in church growth mathematics?

There are! This chapter will attempt to describe seven of them.[1] A particular growing church may not have all these marks. But careful examination of those churches that are experiencing conversion growth—not primarily transfer or biological growth—will reveal a combination of most of these characteristics.

I

Goals

Growing churches know where they are going. They have *growth* goals.

Churches and Goals

In relationship to goals, churches fall into three groups. It is remarkable, but disturbing, that many congregations have no concept of going anywhere. *They set no goals.* Some even insist that goals smack of carnality and evince a lack of trust in God. The truth is that God-honoring, faith-stretching, need-meeting goals are bold affirmations of faith in a living, loving God. Reluctance to set goals often reflects the fear of losing face in case of failure. To handle the fear of failure, these churches say, "Establish no goals!" They are exactly right! Those going nowhere almost always arrive at their destination.

The second group of churches in relationship to goals is the one which *sets only maintenance goals.* Too much theological training today prepares leaders only for a maintenance ministry. The battle cry is, "Hold what you have!" All energy is put into defense. Seldom is the shout, "Possess the land!" proclaimed from the pulpit and then made a priority in goal-setting, the allocation of resources, and the creation of programs. These churches are enslaved by maintenance ministries. They focus all their time and resources on setting up and pumping up institutionalized organizations, fossilized traditions, and antiquated facilities. No time or resources remain for growth.

Take a hard look at your church goals right now. How many are primarily maintenance oriented? How many are aimed at outreach? Which have priority?

The third class of churches are those that *set goals calculated to produce growth*. No local congregation or larger church body in America is consistently experiencing growth without growth goals. Most goals are not met precisely, but they determine direction. Some in the church have a vision of how the future can be. That is a goal.

Use Your Goals

The goals of growing churches *keep purpose and need in proper perspective*. All energies can be given to doing good things—things that *need* to be done—and the church forgets its reason for being. To win men to faith in Christ, gather them into churches, and see them live as responsible disciples of Christ are part of the divine purpose in the world. Growing churches do not lose sight of purpose.

The goals of growing churches *make planning a possibility*. Without goals, planning is impossible. A plan is only a road map to get you from where you are to where you want to be. With an established destination, you can then determine how to get there. Growing churches plan on the basis of established goals.

Growth goals are an *essential part of motivation* in growing churches. Man is so constituted that he is a goal-reaching creature. The mind of man—students of human behavior say—is like the servomechanism on a guided missile. When it is locked on a particular target, it will automatically make corrections and move toward that goal. Goals that are *owned* by an entire church move that church into action.

Goals *become the basis of evaluation* in growing churches. Goals are measurable by definition. With a goal one always knows if it has been reached or how much yet needs to be done. Growing churches constantly use their goals as instruments of review to evaluate their progress in the process of growth.

The big problem faced today in terms of goals is not overoptimism—

setting unrealistic goals. Two other problems overwhelm the churches. First, goals are so small they neither honor God nor challenge men. Then, once goals are set, church leaders and members do not own them with their lives, possessions, and energies. Congregations are only partially committed to goal achievement. To forget them or dilute them produces neither regret nor shame. Only wholehearted commitment to high goals will make them a reality. Growing churches usually have that commitment.

Test Your Goals

A threefold test can be given to any goal to determine its value and desirability.[2] Always test your goals. Ask yourself some questions. Give honest answers. Does your goal honor God? This is the *glory* test. When the goal is achieved, will it be something for which God will be praised? Second, does the goal meet human need? This can be called the *gumption* test. Does it solve a real problem, that confronts real people, in your community today? Does your goal make good sense? Finally, will the goal grip the imaginations and interests of men? This is the *gift* test. Will it create excitement? Will it evoke commitment? Will it call forth the spiritual gifts of the church?

II

Homogeneous Units

Growing churches focus on homogeneous units (HU's).

Understanding Homogeneous Units

A homogeneous unit is any section of society that has at least one characteristic in common. All of us belong to several HUs. You may belong to an HU of bald men over forty. Others may be part of an HU consisting of all the employees of IBM or AT&T. You may be a member of an association of CB operators. All these are HU's.

However, the most permanent and pervasive HU's do not usually relate to physical characteristics, employment, or recreational associations. They are related to kinship, culture, race, and socioeconomic status. If you grew up in Texas and move to Connecticut, you automatically become a member of the Texas Transplants. You feel a kinship to other Texas Transplants that you may not identify with at all while in Texas. If you are from Eastern Kentucky and move to the south side of

Chicago to work in the steel mills, you belong to an HU called Hillbillies. If you move to Houston from Wisconsin or Michigan, you are a member of an HU called Yankees. There is probably an Evangelical Free Church, an American Lutheran Church, or Christian Reformed Church where you could speak English with a Midwestern flavor and remember the snow. These illustrations provide a context for understanding HU's.

Recognizing Homogeneous Units

Language-culture and racial groups form the most obvious and largest HU's. It is often difficult to cross those barriers with the gospel of Christ. To do this effectively in the same congregation is almost impossible.

Socioeconomic distinctions are the most unrecognized homogeneous groupings. There will be many homogeneous subgroups within the Spanish-speaking community or the black community, just as there are in the white, English-speaking majority in America. While distinctive socioeconomic groups may speak the same English dialect and have grown up in the same locale, they are different nevertheless.

No man should be *forced* to cross a language, racial, or socioeconomic barrier to find Christ. He should be able to hear of Christ in his own dialect from his own people, and confess him among his own peers. The recognition of similarities and differences between an individual and a group is often described in terms of comfort. Individuals "feel comfortable" with some groups and "feel uncomfortable" with others. Every man should be invited, but no man should be compelled to become a Christian among people with whom he is uncomfortable.

Nothing causes more distress among American Evangelicals today than to insist that one church in a community cannot serve all segments of society. The statement sounds like racism or snobbery. It violates our theology of church and gospel. It suggests the inadequacy of a local congregation. In short, it makes us angry!

At this point we must be tough minded. Because a church has ten Spanish surname, bilingual families in attendance does not mean it is reaching the Hispanic community. By insisting that the only opportunity the black population in your city has to become church members is in the fellowship of your predominately white congregation effectively keeps some men from Christ. No one has that right!

This does not mean churches should be closed to racial or language groups. A church with a closed door policy cannot call itself a New Testament church. A garbage collector should not be *compelled* to come to Christ in the church where a group of corporation presidents are the principal leaders. Nor should a bank president be forced to find Christ in a church whose leaders are composed primarily of semiliterate ditch diggers. Failure to recognize the various HU's is a tragic oversight for one interested in the growth of the church of Jesus Christ in all segments of society.

Utilizing Homogeneous Units

How then are HU's related to growing churches? Consider, first, the HU created by common employment. When a church finds men or women in its membership employed by Gulf Oil, IBM, or a local hospital, for example, it should get them together; let them get acquainted; ask them about their peers in the company; and encourage the group to develop a prayer and outreach strategy for other employees of that company. These Christians then become bridges between Christ and his church and their fellows.

Some churches, for example, in Northern Illinois have large segments of General Telephone people. There are churches in Houston that have been very successful in penetrating the NASA community.

Extended families are productive HU's for church growth. When a new Christian is welcomed into the church he should be asked immediately about his family. The query should include more than his immediate relatives. Does he have cousins, aunts, brothers, or in-laws in the community? Is there anyone with whom he has a kinship? These people are often most responsive to his witness.

Special care needs to be given to those who come into a church from an HU that is a significant cultural distance from the majority of church members. Consider, for example, a South Vietnamese family in an English-speaking Caucasian church. Tremendous efforts should be made, not only to integrate the family into the church, but also to discover other Vietnamese families who might be reached for Christ through the witness of the Christian family.

In short, find homogeneous units and attempt to penetrate them. Growing churches do this with great success, and often do not even know it.

III

Laity

Growing churches mobilize and train the laity.

There has never been significant growth of the church without the serious involvement of lay persons. Between 1787 and 1795 Baptists became the largest group of Christians in America. They did it without a home mission board or society; a national convention; a state convention; or a seminary. They did it with small missionary associations and lay preachers—most of them were not paid a salary. They were without formal theological training. Most of them had been licensed to exercise their gifts by little Baptist churches. The Presbyterians, Episcopalians, and Congregationalists insisted that they were not clergy at all, but untrained, undisciplined laymen who should be at home working instead of out preaching.

Between 1795 and 1820 the Methodists overtook and surpassed the Baptists in total members. They did it with lay preachers going everywhere sharing their faith, forming disciplined small groups, and gathering churches.

There never has been, nor will there ever be, multiplication of disciples and churches apart from the mobilization of the laity to the work.

Jack Hyles, pastor of First Baptist Church, Hammond, Indiana, has a sermon he sometimes delivers to pastors' conferences entitled "Trotline Fishing." The reason his church has experienced significant growth, he insists, is because he has given up fishing with one hook. In most churches the pastor is the only person who "catches men." In the Hammond church new Christians are added every week because the laity is mobilized. There are many hooks "catching men" throughout the week.

How do you mobilize the laity?

Lay persons are mobilized by a challenge to spiritual, sacrificial, significant ministry. The challenge must be issued through one who is responding to the challenge himself.

Most challenges given to lay Christians today are defective in several ways. They are often *anemic*. Nothing is asked for! No real challenge is involved. No sacrifice is demanded. That which demands no sacrifice is usually ultimately unimportant. Challenges are often only *materialistic*. No spiritual ministry in the name of or for the sake of Jesus Christ can be discovered in the challenge. What is called for cannot be distinguished from the challenge of the United Fund, Red Cross, or Y.M.C.A. fund drives. A *big* challenge in most churches is too often only for something material—a building, a more expensive organ, or better stained glass windows. The need may be real, but the challenge has no breath of heaven on it.

Challenges are often *dull*. They are challenges to meet an organizational need, to fill a spot, to become a little cog in a small wheel that does nothing but go in circles.

Finally, challenges are often only *temporal.* There is nothing of eternal significance in what men and women are asked to do. The task of helping men and women find everlasting life through faith in Jesus Christ is subconsciously considered the domain of the clergy. The challenge given to the laity is mundane and drab.

How do you train the laity?

Believers must first be trained in those things essential to the Christian life. Several questions need to be answered: How can you be personally assured that you are a Christian? How do you handle the problem of sin in your daily life? Who is the Holy Spirit and what is his ministry in your life? How do you maintain a vital relationship with Christ in your daily walk? What is the place and importance of the church?

Believers need to be trained in the disciplines of the Christian life. What is prayer and how do you have a meaningful prayer life? How do you study and apply the Word of God to your personal life? How can you share your life in Christ with other Christians? How can you witness with power to your friends, family, and those you meet?

Finally, believers need to be helped to discover their spiritual gifts, to be trained for exercising those gifts effectively, and then to be turned loose to utilize those gifts for the glory of God and the good of man.

Is there a way to go about this?

We believe there is. It is found in 2 Timothy 2:2: "What you have heard from me before many witnesses entrust to faithful men who will be able to teach others also" (RSV). This was the method of Jesus who invested most of his ministry in twelve men. This is the pattern of the early church. "And they [the 3,000 baptized] devoted themselves to the apostles' teaching and fellowship, to the breaking of bread and the prayers" (Acts 2:42, RSV). Church leaders must take Ephesians 4 very seriously. The saints must be equipped for the work of the ministry.

Looking at the Great Commission (Matthew 28:18–20) from the viewpoint of lay mobilization will suggest a threefold process.[3]

While and wherever we go, Christ's imperative is that we (1) make disciples. As disciples are made, and while we continue to be obedient to that imperative, we are (2) baptizing the new disciples and (3) teaching them to obey him in all things. Making disciples is always the great imperative. While we continue in that process, those disciples newly made are to be added to his church, and developed toward full obedience to his will. Paul expresssed it like this: "I was made a minister . . . that I might fully carry out the preaching of the word of God . . . And we proclaim Him, admonishing every man and teaching every man with all wisdom, that we may present every man complete in Christ" (Col. 1:25–28, NASB). Growing churches have been able to make disciple-makers as well as to make disciples.

A mobilized, motivated, and discipled laity is always a mark of a growing church.

IV

Diversified Ministry

Growing churches have diversified ministries.

Nothing is more obvious, nothing is more universal among growing churches. However, it is equally obvious that a full quiver of ministries in a community does not guarantee growth. Many churches have proliferated programs and ministries within a community, but continue to decline. On what basis then do growing churches diversify?

Ministry diversification, first of all, must be according to the leadership of the Holy Spirit. It is God-given ministries, performed in God-directed ways, for God-established goals that are blessed by heaven. To these ministries God sends the increase. Church leaders should invest time— real, calendared time—to humbling themselves before God and saying, "Lord, what would you have us to do?" When a church commits itself to do only as the Lord God leads, then it can expect him to give direction. The Bible speaks often and clearly: "Trust in the Lord with all your heart, and do not rely on your own insight. In all your ways acknowledge him, and he will make straight your paths" (Prov. 3:5–6, RSV). Diversifying ministries according to the leadership of the Holy Spirit does not imply that his leadership comes by fiat, written on tables of stone. Certain things should always be considered.

Consideration should be given to *felt need* in the community. This needs to be underlined. Not necessarily the universal and eternal needs of man, but local temporal hurts in a given community demand consideration in formulating the ministries of the church.

If you plan to reap a harvest, the soil needs to be tested. Go house to house and attempt to discover those programs for which there is a crying need. Then, under the leadership of God, meet that need.

Consideration should be given to the *gifts* when the church looks for God's direction in new ministries. First Corinthians 12–14 teaches that God has equipped his church to do the work it has been sent to do. The neo-Pentecostal movement has forced other Evangelicals to look seriously at the biblical doctrine of spiritual gifts. Too much dependence has been put on natural talents. We have tended to focus almost all the gifts in one person—the pastor. We have insisted that every Christian should teach, and, if a person is really dedicated, he will be teaching the Bible in our Sunday Schools. This is just as big a mistake as holding that everyone should speak in tongues. When God leads a church into a new ministry, he will have someone in that church to perform that ministry as an expression of his gift.

Finally, consideration should be given to *open doors* into diversifying ministries. This is not to suggest that a church walk through every narrow opening, but when opportunity clearly knocks we should say, "Lord, if this is of you, make it very clear to us. If this is of you, we will step through this door."

Through felt needs, the manifestation of gifts, and open doors, the Holy Spirit leads churches into various growth ministries.

One other word needs to be said. Diversified ministries demand program flexibility. If we are more concerned about maintaining Wednesday night prayer meeting, 9:30 A.M. Bible study, and 7:30 P.M. worship, than we are in following God's leadership through open doors, then we will never be able to produce growing churches.

Without flexibility churches quickly become program-centered instead of God-centered and/or people-centered. The thrust is toward salvaging a structure, sanctifying a program, maintaining a tradition, or perpetuating an institution. Divine obedience is forgotten. The will of God and the need of men are shoved aside in devotion to a cultural expression.

It is almost heresy to say it, but it is nevertheless true. There was a time before Sunday School was. There may be a time when Sunday School is no more. Sunday School as we know it is far different from the Sunday School before 1850. The Sunday School after 2000 A.D. may be entirely different from the one we know today.

Growing churches diversify their ministries. That demands program flexibility.

V

Small Groups

Growing churches utilize small group dynamics.

Small groups, regardless of the anxiety they produce among many contemporary church leaders, are nothing new to the Christian movement. Jesus spent three years in a small group relationship with twelve men. One of them went bad. But the investment of his life in the remaining eleven actually changed history.

Small Group Dynamics

For purposes of church growth, emphasis must be placed on the word *dynamics*. Small groups of people can meet regularly and never experience reproductive, spiritual, vitality. Members may enjoy getting together, sharing with, and caring for one another, but never really know the vigor of a *contagious* common life. It is small group dynamics, not small groups that are related to growing churches.

This dynamic is often employed within very large units of people. Huge churches with thousands of members may have hundreds of small groups that add life-giving vigor to those churches. A Bible class may grow large on the same principle. Organized into small units of sharing and fellowship within the larger class, these small groups may become conductors of life within the larger unit. Just as an extension cord can become a conductor of electrical power as the electrical current flows through its various wires, small groups can become conductors of life power as the life-current of Jesus Christ flows through its various members.

Becoming Life Conductors

How does a group become a conductor of life? By experiencing vital, infectious, spiritual fellowship with Jesus Christ and one another.

The early days of the Jerusalem Church provide the classic example. That young church experienced an authentic spiritual fellowship in which hundreds were added to its number. Acts 2:47, indeed provides an excellent goal statement for a growing church: "And the Lord added to their number day by day those who were being saved" (RSV). When the church experiences infectious fellowship with one another and its Lord, growth most often becomes spontaneous.

Careful study of Acts 2:41–47 will show that the spontaneous growth of this early church was closely related to the dynamics of small groups. At least four ingredients contributed to the contagious and reproductive character of this life.[4]

1. *"They devoted themselves to the apostles' teaching and fellowship"* (Acts 2:42, RSV). What was the "teaching" that is particularly "the apostles'?" It must be that expansion of Old Testament teaching that Jesus spent three years pouring into the twelve. It is the doctrine epitomized on

that unforgettable evening in the upper room on resurrection day. "He opened their minds to understand the scriptures, and said to them, 'Thus it is written, that the Christ should suffer and on the third day rise from the dead, and that repentance and forgiveness of sins should be preached in his name to all nations, beginning from Jerusalem' " (Luke 24:45–47, RSV).

It was the New Testament in miniature, the seed of what was to come.

And what is the apostles' *koinonia?* What else but that fellowship—that brotherhood—that the twelve had known with Jesus for three years? The new believers were introduced to both. It was the Bible, applied in the here and now, giving meaning to present experiences, shared in a small group that was the first ingredient of the spiritual vitality of the early church.

2. *"They devoted themselves . . . to the breaking of bread and the prayers"* (Acts 2:42, RSV). Intimate worship, particularly that represented by the Lord's Supper and prayer, is the second ingredient of the early church's vigor. Where did this "worship" take place? The following verses tell us—"in their homes." The informal, intimate character of worship within the various small groups must be stressed. Breaking the loaf together suggests the unity of these small groups. They were in intimate communion with each other. Prayer suggests direct fellowship with the Father.

3. *"All who believed were together and had all things in common"* (Acts 2:44, RSV). They shared their life together. Too much focus has been given to the selling of property and goods, as if the only thing these early believers shared was material things. They first shared their inner life— the Christ within. They first came to know one another. Then they could share their material things with "glad and generous hearts" (Acts 2:46, RSV).

4. *Finally, these new believers responded to need and opportunity.* Or, to put it another, more positive way, *these believers discovered their own ministries.* They found ways they could begin to express the presence of Christ within. Having received the gift, they had gifts through which to mediate Jesus Christ. For some it was the ministry of giving. Not all had property to sell, else there would have been no need at that point. Need there was. "They began selling their property and possessions, and were sharing them with all, as anyone might have need" (Acts 2:45, NASB).

They also discovered the ministry of evangelism. That is the best way to describe their continual activity, "with one mind," in the Temple. They went there to share the good news with the people gathered in that place.

They went right to the center of greatest opposition. They witnessed right under the noses of those who had put Jesus to death. The events of chapters four and five bear this out. Out of Bible study, prayer and community arose ministry. In short, they had become conductors of life.

Utilization of Small Groups

Small groups can contribute to church growth in several different ways.

1. Time and time again a small group has become an *instrument of renewal* in a local congregation and/or a larger church body.

2. Small groups may themselves become *centers of training* for various ministries.

3. A small group can be an *agent of ministry*, responding to discovered need.

4. But most significantly for church growth, small groups become *cells of outreach* to the world.

Howard A. Snyder, in *The Problem of Wine Skins,* a seminal book on the biblical implications for the structure of the modern church, said, "A small group of eight to twelve people meeting together informally in homes is the most effective structure for the communication of the gospel in modern secular urban society. Such groups are better suited to the mission of the church in today's urban world than are traditional church services, institutional church programs or the mass communication media. Methodologically speaking, the small group offers the best hope for the discovery and use of spiritual gifts and for renewal within the church." [5] In one form or another most growing churches have discovered the power of small group dynamics and have adopted small groups as one of the effective strategies for multiplying and nurturing believers.

VI

Direct Evangelism

Growing churches major on direct evangelism.

Evangelism is one of those words that Christians love and revere but seem utterly unable to define with precision. There is a worldwide debate in Christian circles today between what has been identified as *proclamation* evangelism and *presence* evangelism. Many sincere Christians believe that the evangelistic task worldwide is fundamentally to give everyone a chance to hear. [6] At the other extreme are those who insist that evangelism is primarily expressed in service. If the Christian is only

179

present within the non-Christian world, serving in Jesus' name, he has performed his evangelistic responsibility.

Remarkably, there are advocates of those two views in many evangelical churches today. The only program of evangelism in many churches is an evangelistic campaign or week-long church revival which majors on proclaiming the good news. For many this *is* evangelism and, if a church is not having *event* evangelism, that church is not *evangelistic*. On the other side are those who are badgered and guilty because they have been unable to function effectively as personal soul-winners, or who are worn out and discouraged from trying to get the outsider to attend an evangelistic service. They say, "A good life is the best witness one can give."

Growing churches have gone beyond this debate. They employ evangelistic methods which renounce quietism for enthusiastic verbalization of the good news. They have moved from emphasis only on evangelistic preaching to concerned *persuasion,* to decision, and on to responsible Christian discipleship within the local church.[7] In doing this they have recovered the biblical pattern. Peter not only preached on the day of Pentecost, he also "testified" and "exhorted" with "many other words" (Acts 2:40, RSV). Paul reported that, "knowing the fear of the Lord," he persuaded men, begging them, in behalf of Christ, to be reconciled to God (2 Cor. 5:11,20, RSV). Methods vary, but growing churches always major on direct confrontation of the non-Christians with the claims of Christ and gentle persistence in bringing the new Christian to baptism, fellowship and personal growth within the local congregation.

Evaluation and Pragmatism

If a church is to grow it must be absolutely ruthless in the evaluation of evangelistic methods. Growing churches do not cling to techniques, approaches, or programs that do not work! Traditional methods, no matter how effective in the past, must be examined. How many, during the past five years, have actually been won to Christ from the pagan pool in your community through your spring evangelistic campaign? Is your youth program reaching effectively outside the church family in its evangelistic thrust? How many has it brought to faith in Christ, baptism, and responsible church membership? What about your bus ministry? Is it really adding families to the church? Or, is it recruiting children who make a decision for Christ and then fade back into the unchurched community? Is your Sunday School the outreach and evangelistic organization it is touted to be or does it serve only as an ongoing and not too effective catechetical program that conducts the children of church members from infancy to baptism and church membership?

Be brutally frank with yourself. The New Testament church had neither Sunday School, bus ministry, organized youth program nor eight-day "revivals" that we know about. It did have methods of confronting men with Jesus Christ that were effective. All present methods may need to be continued in your church, but not without fearless evaluation. All must be reshaped and revitalized or utterly abandoned if they do not work. There are multitudes of evangelistic methods. Growing churches are almost always pragmatic. They use methods that work!

Witness and Harvester

Most Evangelicals have been verbally clubbed by their pastors, teachers, and visiting evangelists because they are not aggressively involved in personal evangelism. All members, we have been saying since the first evangelistic canvassing program, should have a ministry of habitual harvesting. One is disobedient to God if he is not successfully achieving that goal.

In reality, the character of a Christian as a *witness* has been confounded with the *evangelistic gift* that the Holy Spirit has given to some people in the church. Every Christian is a witness to what Jesus Christ has done and is doing in his life. But the Holy Spirit has given the evangelistic gift to those in the church as it pleases him. Nor is this gift confined to those traveling preachers we call evangelists. Laymen and women are gifted as well.

All Christians need to be trained to share their witness to Jesus Christ in a clear and winsome manner. They should be given instruction on how to live life at its best, day by day, and be equipped with techniques for communicating to another how he may personally encounter Jesus Christ. Out of that training experience those gifted in evangelism may be helped to discover their gifts.

C. Peter Wagner has asserted—on the basis of considerable evidence—that in most growing churches only about 10 percent of the membership have the potential to become harvesters.[8] In churches that do not grow or grow slightly, less than 1 percent really exercise the evangelistic gift. In many churches only the pastor does that work, and sometimes he is not too effective.

Attention needs to be given to discovering, equipping, and motivating that 10 percent.

Church leaders are uncomfortable about this approach to lay evangelism because they fear that Christians will use the doctrine of spiritual gifts as a cop-out for faithful witnessing. The two need to be clearly distinguished. All members can be trained to bear their witness. The prerequisite is that Jesus Christ is really doing something in their lives to which they can warmly testify. It is unrealistic to expect all witnesses to become harvesters. If a church can discover its gifted band, the work of direct evangelism will go on aggressively.

New Christians are most easily trained to be effective witnesses, and from this group potential harvesters can be identified. Those newly converted to Christ still have direct and healthy relationships with outsiders. Those who have been Christians for many years have fewer meaningful relationships with non-Christians. Thus it is new Christians who have the greatest potential for sharing Christ with the unchurched community.

Just as insurance salesmen in training are often encouraged to make prospective buyers lists from their larger families and close acquaintances, so new Christians should be encouraged to develop a personal witnessing strategy. Non-Christian members of their extended and immediate families and friends and acquaintances within their various homogeneous units to which the new believers belong can be put on a prayer and share list. These people are usually the most responsive to the witness of the young Christian. In this way new homogeneous units can be penetrated with the living Christ.

Maximum evangelistic power in a church is achieved when (1) many believers are able to share a witness to what Jesus is doing in their lives; (2) those with an evangelistic gift are permitted to exercise that gift as their ministry through the church; (3) new believers are immediately involved in sharing their faith with their families and peers.

Adding and Multiplying

In evangelism, growing churches have added multiplication to addition.

Multiplication is a fundamental principle of growth. In no genre of living creatures does growth take place just by one unit adding other units. Some of the added units also begin to add units, while the first unit continues to add other units. That is reproduction by multiplication.

Pastors and congregations are too often brainwashed into believing that church growth must be by addition only. No effort has been made to equip others to reproduce. The pastor or a visiting evangelist are seen as the *only* agents of addition growth.

Multiplication growth takes more time. For new reproducers must be equipped. In the long run, however, multiplication growth is far more productive. Suppose a traveling evangelist visited a church congregation for ten years, and each year 100 new believers were added to the church. In ten years there would be—barring death and transfer—1,000 new members. Suppose one harvester in that church led one person to Christ each year for ten years and trained and equipped him to do the same each year. In five years there would be no contest. The annual evangelistic campaign would add 500 and the lonely harvester and his progeny only thirty-one. But in ten years the total would be 1,000 and 1,073, respectively. In the eleventh year that harvester and his compatriots would add 2,146, and the total would be almost three times as great as the 1,100 added through the evangelistic campaigns.

This example is idealistic, of course, but the principle is valid. Growing churches major on direct evangelism and their goal is multiplication, not just addition growth.

The teachings of Jesus verify this truth. He said to his early disciples, who were by vocation commercial fishermen, "Follow me and I will make you become fishers of men" (Mark 1:17, RSV). Most modern evangelicals who, if they fish at all, fish for sport, have misunderstood the figure Jesus used. They think of a fisherman as a man who uses a rod, line, and lure. Fishing is a one-on-one proposition. In this way, this text has been used to encourage modern Christians to become personal evangelists.

The early disciples fished with nets. Fish were in schools, hopefully, certainly not caught one at a time. Growing churches have captured that vision. They have learned how to fish with nets.

VII

Faith

Growing churches go forward in faith.

No church in America is growing that is convinced that it can't! Faith is *directly* related to church growth. No faith to believe; no power to achieve! It is as simple as that.

That fact shouldn't be surprising or downgraded as civil or folk religion. It is faith as related to righteousness that sets Christianity apart from Judaism (Rom. 3:21–24). We are called to the obedience of faith (Rom. 1:5). Without faith it is impossible to please God (Heb. 11:6). For many Christians, faith is steadfast intellectual and emotional commitment to certain biblical truths. These truths may be called irrational by their pagan peers. But these modern saints hold them tenaciously, the evidence of their faith. Devotion to truth is always commendable and necessary, but faith is more dynamic. "Faith . . . is the confident assurance that some thing we want is going to happen. It is the certainty that what we hope for is waiting for us, even though we cannot see it up ahead" (Heb. 11:1, TLB).

Growing churches have had a revival of believing, of daring to trust God. "Faith as a grain of mustard seed" is all that is needed to move mountains (Matt. 17:20, RSV). Jesus, not Norman Vincent Peale, said, "All things are possible to him who believes" (Mark 9:23, RSV). Jesus, not Maxwell Maltz, said, "All things for which you pray and ask, believe that you have received them, and they shall be granted you" (Mark 11:24, NASB). Jesus, not Robert L. Schuller, said, "Everything you ask in prayer, believing, you shall receive" (Matt. 21:22, NASB). Living to please God requires that we expect great things from God. Expecting much we can attempt much for him.

Growing churches are not lacking in desire, determination, or the confidence that God wants them and will enable them to grow. They are convinced that they have found what God is doing in their community and have joined his team. Doing God's will in God's way at God's time and expecting God's blessing is the obedience of faith.

Thousands of Evangelical churches in America today are on the *pill*. They do not want to grow. Consciously or unconsciously they have repudiated reproduction. There is no burning desire to obey Christ in making disciples of every creature.

Growing churches have *faith to obey*. They believe God has something better for them than stagnation and decline. They desire something better (Heb. 11:8,16). They had rather be thought of as fools, covered up with work, and confronted with new people who often have serious problems, than be disobedient to God.

One of the first things church leaders discover when their church starts to grow is that many members do not want growth. These, often very spiritual Christians, had rather be disobedient to God than to receive strange people into their fellowship, wrestle with the problems growth produces, and/or pay the price in life that growth, or obedience to God, demands.

Growing churches renounce that position and in faith go on to obedience to God.

Growing churches have *faith to count*. They count on the resources of God rather than the circumstance and situation which confront them. They take seriously, not only the commands of God, but the promises of

God. When Jesus cursed the fig tree (Mark 11:12–14), he was not giving vent to petty anger. "It was not the season for figs" (v. 13). He wanted to teach a most important lesson about the place of faith in the life of the Christian. Peter gave him the opportunity the following morning. "Master, look! The fig tree which you cursed has withered." And Jesus answered them, "Have faith in God. Truly, I say to you, whoever says to this mountain, 'Be taken up and cast into the sea,' and does not doubt in his heart, but believes that what he says will come to pass, it will be done for him. Therefore I tell you, whatever you ask in prayer, believe that you received it, and you will" (Mark 11:21–24, RSV).

These words of Jesus seem incredible to most modern Evangelicals. This concept is often called hocus-pocus, self-deception, self-hypnosis, positive thinking, or heresy. But these *are* the words of Jesus.

Robert L. Schuller has pointed out that the proverb, "I'll believe it when I see it," is, according to Jesus, backwards, upside down, and wrong. The statement of faith is *"I'll see it when I believe it."* [9] Growing churches believe the promises of God and count on God keeping them in their behalf.

Growing churches have *faith to try*. They begin! When they have begun, they keep on trying. They will not quit. Discouragements, disappointments, and early defeats are as predictable as sunrise.

Graceland Baptist Church, New Albany, Indiana grew from an average Sunday School attendance of eighty in 1963 to 1,400 in 1976. One of their methods was a bus ministry. They began with one bus and in 1976 had a fleet of fifty. Originally designed only to pick up children for Sunday School, this bus ministry has become a seven day a week program. Free bus service is provided for senior citizens to shopping centers and doctor's offices. They are used as chapels in some communities. Buses are a basic tool in the large "Keen-agers" program for senior adults that the church conducts. The buses added numbers to the church. One large bus route during its first week brought in only thirteen people. Disappointment has been turned into achievement by those who had faith to begin and then refused to quit.[10]

Now give yourself this test.

1. Do we (your church) have clearly defined growth goals? Are our resources (human, material, and financial) really concentrated on reaching those goals?

2. Have you identified the basic homogeneous unit in your church? Have you isolated others in your community? Are you attempting to penetrate them?

3. What percent of the laity in your church is really mobilized? Be honest. One percent, 5 percent, 10 percent, 15 percent, _____ percent? What are you doing to train lay leaders for growth ministries? What are you doing to motivate and mobilize others?

4. Do you have any other ministries besides Bible study, evangelistic worship and revivals? Are these other ministries *really* turned toward outreach? Have you asked yourself what your church could do to minister to the hurting needs of your area?

5. Do you have small groups? Are you opposing them or utilizing them?

6. What kinds of evangelism is your church doing? Is it really effective? How many people were added through your evangelism program last year from the unchurched community in your town?

7. What is your faith quotient? Are you dreaming any faith dreams? Are you asking God for them and planning as if they were sure to come? Are you really expecting God to do anything miraculous in your church?

10
God Wants You to Win!

This book is intended to be a challenge to bold discipleship and bold disciple making. We believe both are a part of the intention of the Father for all his children. God has not purposed that churches stagnate and decline. It is not his plan that his people experience constant defeat and never know the joy of achievement. Jesus came, he said, to provide abundant life. He did not intend that churches or individual believers live in failure and frustration. For that reason Jesus Christ ascended to heaven, and the Holy Spirit was poured out. The Spirit is now present to endow the disciples of Jesus with power for effective witness and ministry.

The first nine chapters of this book have been focused on churches. We want to address this last chapter to you as individual believers and responsible members of some local congregation. We bring you *good* news. God wants you to win! He wants you to be successful in living the Christian life. He wants your church to be successful in fulfilling its mission in the world. Do you want this success he has planned for you?

What Is Success?

Immediately, when the word "success" is used, or one of its derivatives, many modern Christians get up tight. "Success" is a "b-a-a-a-a-d" word! The word is in disfavor because we have defined success in terms of wealth, prestige, and the power that goes with them. We know too many people who have all these things and are total failures. They have missed life!

What is success? We believe it is related to the fact of a person doing what he is created to do or an object doing what it is created to do. A lamp that will not burn, not matter how well it fits the room decor nor how often it stimulates conversation, is a failure. It was created to give light. Success is a combination of being and doing. Just being a lamp is not enough. It must illuminate. It's reason for being must be actualized. So, it is with the individual believer. He or she must be and do what he or she was created to be and do.

Many define success as the achievement of goals. But this is an inadequate definition. Goals can be too low. A man may reach every goal of his life and be an absolute failure. Another person may never quite achieve his goals and, yet, all along the way, he has been successful. Because these observations are true, Ted W. Engstrom asserts success means a person is reaching the maximum potential available to him at any given moment.[1] Wayne Dehoney defines success as "the progressive realization of a person's worthwhile, predetermined goals."[2]

We insist that success is a *good* word. God wants us to be and do what he made us to be and do. He wants us to complete what he sent us to accomplish. God wants you as an individual to progressively realize your worthwhile, predetermined goals. He wills that you reach the maximum potential available to you at each given moment of your life. He wants you to win. He wants you to win in every facet of your life—spiritual, emotional, physical, mental, and vocational.

Success Principles

Are there success principles? We believe there are. In an effort to discover those maxims of success that are most relevant to the disciple of Jesus Christ, especially as he relates to the growth of the church, we decided to examine the life of the most influential church growth specialist who ever lived. If we could find those factors that explain his life, we might find instructions for our own.

The apostle Paul was the subject of our study. Lots of material was available in *Acts* and the personal narratives in his letters. These paragraphs pull back the curtain from his life and help us understand what really made him tick. Paul made a habit of success. We found that this habit was undergirded by an attitude of achievement as well as strong attributes of character and personality.

I

Three Steps Toward the Mind of a Winner

In one amazing passage Paul unveils something of the philosophy of success. "Do you not know that those who run in a race all run, but only one receives the prize? Run in such a way that you may win. And everyone who competes in the games exercises self-control in all things.

They then do it to receive a perishable wreath, but we an imperishable. Therefore I run in such a way, as not without aim; I box in such a way, as not beating the air; but I buffet my body and make it my slave, lest possibly, after I have preached to others, I myself should be disqualified" (1 Cor. 9:24–27, NASB).

Three ideas jump out of this paragraph which can help you advance toward the mentality of a winner.

1. *Develop a winning attitude.* Paul refers to the games customarily held in the Greco-Roman world. Our own Olympic games have them as a model. Of course, only one contestant wins each event. But, Paul went on to say, "Run in such a way that you may win."

That short sentence is the heart of what he had to say. "Win or lose, get in the race and run as if you intended to win." In other words, "Think win!" Reject ideas of failure and defeat. You will not be successful in every situation. But, at least, run the race like you expected to finish in the winner's circle. Nothing is so urgent to the mind of a winner than an attitude that expects achievement.

Mankind has rediscovered an amazing truth during the last century. *Men can change their attitudes of mind.* We do not have to be enslaved by situations and circumstances. Victor Frankl, who survived Auschwitz, has become one of the most respected psychotherapists of all time. He observed human life, his own and others, at the extremes of endurance. We who lived in concentration camps [he wrote] can remember the men who walked through the huts comforting others, giving away their last piece of bread . . . . They offer sufficient proof that everything can be taken from a man but one thing: the last of human freedoms—to choose one's attitude in any given set of circumstances, to choose one's own way? [3]

That was a truth that Paul knew well. For that reason he urged believers to throw themselves into the Christian life with a mind to win.

2. *Determine specific goals.* The RSV translates 1 Corinthians 9:26 brilliantly. "Well, I do not run aimlessly." That is one of the keys to the mind of Paul. He was never goalless; he was always goal-oriented. His goals were always in line with the overarching purposes of God. He knew who he was and what he was sent to do.

The life of modern man is often characterized by meaninglessness. This is true, students of human behavior say, because there is no tension between what one has already achieved and what one still ought to accomplish. What man actually needs is not a tensionless state but rather the striving and struggling of some goal worthy of him. [4]

This condition in human society has infected churches. Meaninglessness has cast its shadow over believers and whole congregations. There is no tension between the contemporary *is* and the divine *ought*. Christians are often like gerbils on exercise wheels. We run, run, run, until we are exhausted. We make a lot of noises, but we go nowhere.

Therefore, a second step to developing the mind of a winner is to set your mind on those "worthwhile, predetermined goals" that you have dared, nudged by the Holy Spirit, to visualize with your creative imagination. Decide on specific, concrete goals for your life and pursue them.

3. *Discover the value of discipline.* For most Christians, real discipline is something to be avoided, not something to be desired. Only those who have made the discovery of the value of discipline ever really succeed. To be what you are and accomplish what you were sent to do demands that you come under the authority of the risen Christ. That submission is discipline.

Paul made that discovery, "I buffet my body and make it my slave" (v. 27, NASB).

It is easy, almost natural, to become a slave to your appetites. Many Christian leaders have so limited the lordship of Christ in their lives they are in bondage to one or more of the God-given drives that constitute life itself. Sin, Peter Lord has said so well, is nothing more than using a God-given drive in a God forbidden way. The value of discipline is that it puts the body as well as the spirit of the believer at the disposal of Christ.

The word *discipline*, obviously, is closely related to "discipleship." Success in the Christian life, or true discipleship, waits on discipline. Discipline denies the fragmentation of the use of energy that is so characteristic of many Christians. It permits the balanced, intensive focus on being and achieving. This is the stuff of a winning life. It keeps us from those habits or entanglements that could cause us to be "disqualified" and hinder us from achieving the divine intention for the life of the believer. It makes concentration on the essential and the necessary possible. It undergirds habitual accomplishment.

II

Six Traits Essential to a Winning Habit

Paul not only had a winning attitude; his character and personality were marked by six traits that can guarantee significant achievement in the Christian life.

1. *Paul had one life-consuming ambition—to know Christ.*

But whatever gain I had, I counted as loss for the sake of Christ. Indeed I count everything as loss because of the surpassing worth of knowing Christ Jesus my Lord. For his sake I have suffered the loss of all things, and count them as refuse, in order that I may gain Christ and be found in him, not having a righteousness of my own . . . but that which is through faith in Christ . . . that I may know him and the power of his resurrection, and may share his sufferings, becoming like him in his death, that if possible I may attain the resurrection from the dead (Phil. 3:7–11, RSV).

How do you get to know someone?

There is really only one way. Spend time with him; interact with him; speak to him; let him speak to you. Have dealings with each other. The same requirements apply to knowing the risen Christ that apply to knowing anyone else. There is no available short cut for really knowing any person.

Personal knowledge demands the investment of time with another. That is why we have elaborate and sometimes extended courtship procedures before marriage. People, we say in America, should know each other before they marry. Two people about to get married usually have invested hours in getting to know each other.

A continued intimate relationship demands more hours alone. Many marriages are in trouble today because two people who invested days in getting acquainted, before and immediately after marriage, have become so involved in the duties of marriage and vocation that they never spend time with each other. Many Christians are estranged from a personal, intimate, daily walk with Christ for the same reasons. Personal, intimate acquaintance, even for people who have been married for years, demands time together alone. Regardless of how long one has known Christ, time alone with him is essential for knowing him.

The first maxim to a life of Christian achievement is to get to know Christ. Make that the first priority of your life. That only is possible through time alone with him.

2. *Paul had a fantastic, God-given dream.* He was a man obsessed with a grand theme, a big objective, an amazing goal. He spelled it out in his letter to the Ephesian Christians. "To me, though I am the very least of all the saints, this grace was given, to preach to the Gentiles the unsearchable riches of Christ, and to make all men see what is the plan of the mystery hidden for ages in God who created all things; that through the

church the manifold wisdom of God might now be made known to the principalities and powers in the heavenly places" (Eph. 3:8–10, RSV).

His dream was threefold: (1) to preach Christ to the Gentiles; (2) to help all men understand the eternal plan of God; and (3) to be a part of making the wisdom of God manifest to heavenly rulers and authorities. No little dream for Paul! He was in the flow of the eternal purpose of God in Christ Jesus. He saw himself as an important part of the divine purpose.

Every person who has ever achieved anything worthwhile has had a dream. A big, mind-expanding, energy begetting gift-evoking, time-consuming, life-demanding, dream is essential to major achievement in any field. If the Holy Spirit does wonderful things through your life, one of the first things he will do is lay hold of you with a dream.

The ball-and-chain that cripples and confines the average believer today is he dreams small dreams or no dreams. In an age when young men are to see visions and old men are to dream dreams, modern Christians slumber with emasculated imaginations and are afflicted with spiritual myopia.

You cannot achieve, and God cannot achieve through you, more than you can dream. So dream big dreams. If you can't dream it, you can't do it.

Some Christians are troubled by these assertions at two points. First, they say with commendable humility, "God may not have big plans for me. I'm not anything. I'm nothing and I have no desire to be famous or successful." If you are one of those, our first response is that you are, of course, correct. You are nothing. Only one of those for whom Christ died. You are only one of those in whom God invested the life of his Son. You are nothing? Only one chosen in Christ before the foundation of the world. You are only one of those predestined to be conformed to the image of his Son. You are extremely important to God! "Why, even the hairs of your head are all numbered" (Luke 12:7, RSV). You are nothing? Where did you ever get that idea? God did not give it to you.

Furthermore, we are not talking about being famous except in the pursuit and performance of the will of God. We believe God wants each of us to reach his full potential, beginning right now, and to progressively attain, through the rest of his life, those worthwhile goals that are part of his plan for you. To do that requires a dream.

Secondly, some Christians are honestly fearful their dreams may not be from God. "How do I know whether the dream I have is from God or is my own self-centered, self-willed creation, the product of a fertile but carnal mind?"

We have repeatedly insisted that our minds must be brought in submission to Christ. It is easy for the Christian to become preoccupied with *his* dreams, *his* aspiration, *his* own little bailiwick, and miss the perfect plan of God for his life. Thought, word, and deed must be placed under the control of the Spirit. Christ's Lordship must have comprehensive and practical application to your life.

We remind you, however, that God does have a unique and wonderful plan for your life. He has a more amazing plan for you than you could ask for or imagine. You cannot possibly dream a more wonderful dream that the one God has for you. You would do better to pray, "Lord expand my mind so that I can dream just half of what you want to do in and through me in Jesus Christ." Paul concluded Ephesians 3 with these words: "Now to him who by the power at work within *us* is able to do far more abundantly than all that we ask or think, to him be glory in the church and in Christ Jesus to all generations, for ever and ever" (Eph. 3:20–21, RSV).

Amen! Give yourself to a God-given dream.

3. *Paul had a lifelong strategy.* He was a man with a plan. His commitment to planning is evident from many points of view. He developed and utilized a strategy for planting and growing churches throughout his ministry. Probably the best example of it is his ministry in Ephesus. "He entered the synagogue and for three months spoke boldly, arguing and pleading about the kingdom of God; but, when some were stubborn . . . he withdrew . . . and argued daily in the hall of Tyrannus. This continued for two years, so that all the residents of Asia heard the word of the Lord, both Jews and Greeks" (Acts 19:8–10, RSV).

Those who were won to Christ in his daily, public evangelistic ministry were gathered into house churches all over the city (Acts 20:20). When these new disciples had some maturity and had been equipped, they were sent out to the other cities and villages of Asia (Col. 1:7).

The importance of a definite strategy for Paul can also be seen in the pattern of his personal ministry. Paul did not misuse time. He summarized his strategy and the work pattern that activated it when he spoke to the elders from Ephesus. "You yourselves know [he said] how I lived among you all the time from the first day that I set foot in Asia, serving the Lord with all humility and with tears and with trials . . . how I did not shrink from declaring to you anything that was profitable, and teaching you in public and from house to house, testifying both to Jews and to Greeks of repentance to God and of faith in our Lord Jesus Christ" (Acts 20:18–21, RSV).

Fundamental to his plan of missionary extension and his pattern of ministry was a life-long, personal strategy that shaped his approach to life.

> For though I am free from all men, I have made myself a slave to all, that I might win the more. To the Jews I became as a Jew, that I might win Jews; to those under the law, I became as one under the law—though not being myself under the law—that I might win those under the law. To those outside the law, I became as one outside the law—not being without law toward God but under the law of Christ—that I might win those outside the law. To the weak I became weak, that I might win the weak. I have become all things to all men, that I may by all means save some (1 Cor. 9:19–22, RSV).

We will not attempt exposition of this paragraph. It is troubling for many Christians. When Paul said, "I have become all things to all men that I might by all means save some" (v. 22), he certainly was not advocating a policy of evangelistic expediency. To the same group of Christians he insisted that he had renounced disgraceful and under-handed ways. "We refuse to practice cunning or to tamper with God's word, but by the open statement of the truth we . . . commend ourselves to everyman's conscience in the fear of God" (see 2 Cor. 4:2).

This statement about his personal strategy (1 Cor. 9:19–22) contains three ideas that are extremely important if one is to make a habit of winning against those forces that would keep the Church from growing.

First, Paul occupied the *role of a servant*. Not only was he a servant of God, he made himself a servant to man. This aspect in the life of Paul has been overlooked by many modern believers. In this, Paul was doing no more than follow in the footsteps of his Master.

Reading the personal narrative of Paul illustrates that he actually functioned in the role of servant. "You yourselves know," he said to people who did know, "that these hands ministered to my necessities, and to those who were with me. In all things I have shown you that by so toiling one must help the weak" (Acts 20:34–35, RSV).

Do you want to be successful in what God has sent you to do? Every morning when you get up, ask God (and yourself) what you can do *that day* to *serve* people. The seeds of real service inevitably bear the fruit of achievements.

Secondly, Paul's life strategy was one that *adapted to the situation of his audience*. In modern merchandising terms, Paul's product (his message and ministry) was customer-centered. He was sensitive to people culturally, socially, and psychologically. He did not make people cross barriers to hear the good news. He crossed barriers to them. He found where *they* were and went to *them.*

The last two thousand years of Christian history are filled with illustrations of churches that would not cross barriers to waiting people, hungry for the message of Christ. Instead, they said, "If those people want to be Christians, let them come to our building, hear the gospel in our language, and live by our cultural standards." The Judaizers were the forerunners of a great host that have refused to adapt culturally and socially. They have spawned strategies of eventual failure.

A life strategy that wins is one that says, "I will change for you and for the sake of the gospel."

Finally, Paul's life strategy was *essentially evangelistic.* Do not overlook this. "To win," "to save" was integral to Paul's life. This does not mean that Paul's service had strings attached or that his adaptation was, after all, only manipulative. Those are modern charges by persons who wish to disparage and ridicule the evangelistic task of churches. Rather, Paul served and adapted out of obedience to Christ. He had received a divine commission to go to the Gentiles, to turn them "from darkness to light and from the power of Satan to God" (Acts 26:16–18, RSV). Thus he could write: "For we are not, like so many, peddlers of God's word; but as men of sincerity, as commissioned by God, in the sight of God we speak in Christ" (2 Cor. 2:17, RSV).

Paul served people and adapted to people culturally so that he could be *more* effective evangelistically. His goal was to do what was necessary "to win the more" (1 Cor. 9:19, RSV).

The commission of the risen Christ given to Saul of Tarsus is no different from that which he gave to the church and to you. If you want a winning habit in the Christian life, adapt a lifelong personal strategy that focuses on people where they are, sets out to serve people in their needs and aims at nothing less than personal faith in and allegiance to Jesus Christ.

4. *Paul had boundless dedication.* That much is evident by looking at the details of his life. His ministry was characterized by gargantuan labors that often included extreme hardships. In a time when it was necessary to defend his ministry he wrote:

Are they servants of Christ? I am a better one—(I am talking like a madman)—with far greater labors, far more imprisonments, with countless beatings, often near death. Five times I have received at the hands of the Jews the forty lashes less one. Three times I have been beaten with rods; once I was stoned. Three times I have been shipwrecked; a night and a day I have been adrift at sea; on frequent journeys, in danger from rivers, danger from robbers, danger from my own people, danger from Gentiles, danger in the city, danger in the wilderness, danger at sea, danger from false brethren; in toil and hardship, through many a sleepless night, in hunger and thirst, often without food, in cold and exposure. And apart from other things, there is the daily pressure upon me of my anxiety for all the churches" (2 Cor. 11:23–28, RSV).

Paul knew the short spelling of "dedication" is W-O-R-K. There is no substitute for it. Dedication means labor of mind and muscle. Thus, Paul could say, "For this [proclaiming Christ and presenting every man mature in him] I toil, striving with all the energy which he mightily inspires within me" (Col. 1:29, RSV).

We have alluded often in this book to the ministry of the Holy Spirit. The growth that comes from God is only produced by him. The Christian should be filled, controlled, and led by the Spirit of God. It is essential that Christians discover how to walk and witness in the Spirit. Nonetheless, it is gross misunderstanding of what it means to be filled with the Holy Spirit to believe that achievement will come without physical exertion. To be filled with the Holy Spirit is nothing more than to be filled with and controlled by Jesus Christ. Jesus Christ was neither lazy nor inactive. He often knew severe physical exhaustion. Just to break bread and fish to feed 5,000 men, plus women and children was an enormous physical task.

The high road on which a believer walks in the Spirit is bordered by two rough and hazardous side roads. Many Christians spend most of their lives on one of those side roads.

Call the first the road of *carnal activism*. Those who travel on this road work for Jesus Christ in their own strength. By the dint of their own personality, energy, talents or organizational genius they do what they do. Much is often achieved by those who are most gifted. Hard work and good sense will accomplish much, even with few natural talents. But *carnal activism* is not the intention of God for the normal Christian life. Jesus Christ does not want us to work for him; he wants us to permit him to live and work again *through* us. He wants to continue his mighty works in our physical bodies. The wonderful possibility open to each Christian is Jesus Christ living anew and afresh in his mortal flesh (2 Cor. 4:7–11).

Very often, however, those who come to despair of what is achieved through human effort, no matter how dedicated, and experience the renewal of life in the Spirit, go all the way over the second frontage road. Call it the road of *spiritual passivism*. Those who travel this road only coast. They insist the Christian can do nothing and that Jesus Christ does not want him to try. These Christians no longer go; they wait. If God wants to do something through them he will do it without their plans or efforts.

Both these philosophies of the Christian life are in error. Not carnal activism or spiritual passivism, but spiritual activism is the norm of the Christian life. Death to the self-way, denial of the claims of the "old man," and active, immediate, determined obedience to the word of God and the leadership of the Spirit is the essence of dedication. This always manifests itself in labor, one of the traits of the winning habit. Paul said: "By the grace of God I am what I am, and his grace toward me was not in vain. On the contrary, I worked harder than any of them [the other apostles], though it was not I , but the grace of God which is with me" (1 Cor. 15:10, RSV).

5. *Paul had unquenchable desire*. He would not quit. Obstruction became the occasion for greater effort, more determined prayer and more confident faith.

His desire was motivated by compassion. His was the will to serve not the will to power. His best known words concern his own people. "My heart's desire and prayer to God for them is that they may be saved" (Rom. 10:1, RSV). He also said to Timothy: "*I endure everything* for the sake of the elect, that they also may obtain the salvation which in Christ Jesus goes with eternal glory" (2 Tim. 2:10, RSV).

From this point of view, Paul's words about love read like a personal assessment and reminder for his own life. "If I speak in the tongues of men and of angels, but have not love, I am a noisy gong or a clanging cymbal. And if I have prophetic powers, and understand all mysteries and all knowledge, and if I have all faith, so as to remove mountains, but have not love, I am nothing. If I give away all I have, and if I deliver my body to be burned, but have not love, I gain nothing" (1 Cor. 13:1–3, RSV).

Desire and dedication motivated by anything less than love are sub-Christian.

Unquenchable desire manifests itself in *determined persistence*. Nothing not even death itself, is a deterrent to obedience to God and an evangelical passion for men. "I do not account my life of any value nor as precious to myself [he said], if only I may accomplish my course and the ministry which I received from the Lord Jesus, to testify to the gospel of the grace of God" (Acts 20:24, RSV).

Paul threw himself totally into the task of his life. This is one of the factors that contributed to consistent accomplishment. It is a trait necessary to the winning habit today. People are defeated in life not because of lack of ability, but because they do not give one hundred percent of themselves. They do not put their heart into what they do, which is another way to say they are less than fully given to their tasks. Results do not come to the person who refuses to give himself for the desired results.

A major key to success in any endeavor, to reaching that goal which you deeply desire, is to totally turn loose of yourself and throw all you are into the job or project in which you are involved. "Whatever you are doing, give it all you've got. Give every bit of yourself. Hold nothing back. Life cannot deny itself to the person who gives life his all." [5]

Robert L. Schuller has developed and distributed all over America what he calls the Possibility Thinkers' Creed. It is expressive of this character trait in the apostle Paul. You would do well to memorize it and make it an important part of your life.

> When faced with a mountain
> I will not quit!
>
> I will keep on striving until
> I climb over, find a pass through,
> tunnel underneath . . .
>
> Or simply stay and
> turn the mountain into a GOLD MINE,
>
> WITH GOD'S HELP!

6. *Paul had total confidence that he would be successful in what God had sent him to do.* He expected God to achieve through him. He refused to harbor doubts and cuddle thoughts of failure. He expected to be effective in that for which he had been gifted. This is to say that a major facet of the winning habit of Paul was *faith*. Paul's great confession of this confidence has been memorized by other believers through the centuries. "I can do all things through Him who strengthens me" (Phil. 4:13, NASB).

Paul was confident that wherever God sent him and in whatever circumstances he found himself, God would always enable him to win. "Thanks be to God," he wrote, "who in Christ always leads us in triumph, and through us spreads the fragrance of the knowledge of him everywhere" (2 Cor. 2:14). God had begun the work of grace in him, and he was confident that he would not quit until it was brought to completion (Phil. 1:6).

Usually we think that faith is revealed only in right doctrine and moral behavior. These two evidences are certainly important. Faith which contributes to a winning habit in the life of a Christian is evident in other ways as well.

Paul's faith was revealed in his *steadfast commitment to high principles and worthy objectives.* He lived by high ideals. His principles were not to be compromised. Objectives were not to be diluted. Commitment to principle caused him to rebuke Peter to his face (Gal. 2:11). Commitment to worthy objectives kept him obedient to his commission no matter what it required. "As servants of God," he said, "we commend ourselves in every way: through great endurance, in afflictions, hardship, calamities, beatings, imprisonments, tumults, labors, watching, [and] hunger" (2 Cor. 6:4–6, RSV). Paul held tenaciously to the one high goal. Forgetting what had gone before, he strained forward toward the future. He "pressed on toward the goal for the prize of the upward call of God in Christ Jesus" (Phil. 3:14, RSV). Faith that wins is faith that will not be *derailed.*

Paul's faith was revealed in his *behavior under adverse and extreme conditions.* He was never a victim of circumstances; he was consistently a victor over circumstances. Circumstances were rejected as messengers of *sure* defeat. Circumstances were accepted as the occasion for achievement. This explains, in part, how Paul and Silas could sing praises in prison. They were confident that, no matter what happened to them, God was going to enable them to plant a church in Phillippi. He had expressly sent them to Macedonia to bring the good news. "As far as I am concerned," Paul reported to that same church years later, "I have come to learn, in the circumstances in which I am placed, to be independent of these and self-sufficient. I know in fact how to discipline myself in lowly circumstances. I know in fact how to conduct myself when I have more than enough. In everything and in all things I have learned the secret . . . to have more than enough and to lack. I am strong for all things in the One who constantly infuses strength in me" (Phil. 4:11–13, Wuest).

Shortly after his long ministry in Ephesus had collapsed in one day of violent rioting, Paul repeatedly assured his friends in Corinth, "We do not lose heart" (2 Cor. 4:1,16, RSV). Faith that wins is faith that will not be *depressed.*

Paul's faith was revealed in his *optimistic expectations for tomorrow.* When one door closed, he looked for a bigger, wider door a little further down the road. In time of trouble, pressure or despair, he looked for the purpose of God. In fact, for Paul, one of the fringe benefits of being in

Christ was that it gave purpose to suffering. Human beings tend to endure anything if there is some reason for doing it. Paul had found, through Christ, a meaning in suffering and trouble. Christians can have the highest motive for suffering in serving Christ. Paul sets this in clearest perspective: "We also exult in our tribulations; knowing that tribulation brings about perseverance; and perseverance, proven character; and proven character, hope; and hope does not disappoint, because the love of God has been poured out within our hearts" (Rom. 5:3–5, NASB). Paul could admonish Christians to do as he did. "Give thanks in all circumstances" (2 Thess. 5:18, RSV).

The bitter disappointment that followed the Ephesian riot, when he had to leave a long-term, exciting, and effective place of ministry, was a laboratory in which Paul had to demonstrate once again the triumph of Christ through faith. He put faith to work. Second Corinthians needs to be read from this point of view. He refused to be dismayed. He found renewal for his inner man day by day. "Momentary affliction," he said, "is preparing for us an eternal weight of glory" (2 Cor. 4:17, RSV). He refused to look at the obvious and the temporal. He kept his eyes on the hidden and the eternal. "So," he continued, "we are always of good courage . . . for we walk by faith, not by sight. . . . We make it our aim to please him" (2 Cor. 5:6–9, RSV).

The same faith available to Paul is available to you. In fact, if you are in Christ, you already have it. It may be small, but little faith can move mountains (Matt. 17:20). Begin to exercise the faith you have. Believe God. "Trust in the Lord with all your heart, and do not rely on your own insight. In all your ways acknowledge him, and he will straight make your paths" (Prov. 3:5–6, RSV).

You are born to win when you are born again. The new birth provides you with the primary resource necessary to win as a servant of Christ . . . . the power of the God of the universe.

The new birth is the beginning and the life-style that follows pursues dependence, independence, and interdependence. A winner continually learns to properly balance each of these in his life. He depends on sources beyond himself, but is careful not to fear his own resources. He refuses to give authority over him to those who would enslave him to lesser tasks than those to which he feels called to perform. This independence does not lead him to isolation, but to integration. He knows he cannot win alone. He is dependent on God, others, timing, and certain resources. A winner shares the credit of victory with those who helped bring it about.

The new birth is the result of a surrender. The winning Christian is a surrendered servant of Jesus Christ. His time, dreams, strategy, dedication, desire, and faith grow from roots planted deeply in the nourishing soil of knowing Jesus Christ as Savior and Lord. Knowing Christ means knowing how to surrender. Surrender to Christ is the beginning place for being a Christian winner. From time to time remind yourself to "reactivate the dynamic quality of confidence based on the realistic fact that you have the knowledge and the ability to do what needs doing. And furthermore, you know how to do it competently." [6]

Notes

1. Alan R. Tippett, *Solomon Islands Christianity: A Study in Growth and Obstruction* (London: Lutterworth Press, 1967). The second printing (South Pasadena, California: William Carey Library, n.d.) has been used in this reference, pp. 30–32.

2. Orlando E. Costas, "Depth in Evangelism—An Interpretation of 'In-Depth Evangelism' Around the World," in J. D. Douglas, ed., *Let the Earth Hear His Voice* (Minneapolis, Minnesota: World Wide Publications, 1975), pp. 675–94, contains a full discussion of these concepts.

3. Orlando E. Costas, *The Church and Its Mission: A Shattering Critique from the Third World* (Wheaton, Illinois: Tyndale House Publishers, Inc., 1974), pp. 88–90.

4. *Ibid.*, p. 89.

Chapter 1

1. Hans-Ruedi Weber, "God's Arithmetic," in *Mission Trends No. 2*, Gerald H. Anderson and Thomas F. Stransky, eds. (New York: Paulist Press, 1975), p. 66.

2. The following four types of church growth were identified and illustrated by C. Peter Wagner, in a lecture delivered at Garden Grove Community Church, Garden Grove, California, August 28, 1975.

3. A full discussion of the various types of evangelism can be found in Ralph D. Winter's, "The Highest Priority: Cross-cultural Evangelism," in *Let the Earth Hear His Voice*, J. D. Douglas, ed. (Minneapolis, Minnesota: World Wide Publications, 1975), pp. 213–41. "People blindness" is his term, p. 221.

4. Internal Growth is descriptive of the maturational dimension of church growth identified in the Foreword. It is included here, however, because numerical growth should actually occur within the maturational process. Witness and evangelism must take place in a church's growth toward maturity if the children of members are to be led to faith in Christ and added to the body. By virtue of their family relationship they are already, in a fashion, a part of the inner church family. This insider's relationship sets them apart from those men, women, and children who are in the world.

5. *E-0 evangelism* is not mentioned in Winter's paper. This concept was iden-

tified to the authors at the Church Growth Conference, Springfield, Illinois, February 1975, by Donald A. McGavran.

6. When there is any significant cultural barrier between people, an entirely different set of circumstances exists in reference to the communication of the gospel. There is a great deal of difference between an English-speaking, Anglo-Saxon, American Christian witnessing to a Spanish-speaking American and that same Christian attempting to witness effectively to a cluster of Vietnamese refugee families. The English-speaking and Spanish-speaking Americans are both Americans, and their languages are both European and have many similar words. That kinship does not exist between the American and Vietnamese culture. These two situations are the distinction between *E-2* and *E-3 evangelism*.

Chapter 2

1. Statistical Abstract of the United States (1974), Table #41.
2. *Ibid.*
3. Ralph W. Neighbour, Jr., *The Seven Last Words of the Church, We Never Did It That Way Before* (Grand Rapids: Zondervan, 1972).
4. Robert H. Schuller, *Your Church Has Real Possibilities*, (Glendale, California: G/L Publications, 1975), p. 46.
5. Functional Validity Test. See Appendix Exhibit A.
6. Richard Sprague, *McCalls Magazine*, March 1977, p. 158.
7. Time Use Form. See Manual CGF.
8. Paul Hershey, and Kenneth H. Blanchard, *Management of Organizational Behaviour*, (Englewood Cliffs, New Jersey: Prentice Hall, 1972), p. 36.

Chapter 3

1. *Webster's New Collegiate Dictionary* (1953), s.v. "Principle."
2. W. L. Howse and W. O. Thomason, *The Dynamic Church* (Nashville: Convention Press, 1969), p. 52.
3. Donald McGavran and Win Arn, *How To Grow a Church*, (Glendale: G/L Publications, 1973), pp. 89–92.
4. Rick Gore, "The Awesome World Within Cells," *National Geographic*, Vol. 150, No. 3, September 1976.
5. Schuller, Lyle, *The Change Agent* (Nashville: Abingdon Press, 1972), pp. 64–65.
6. Glasse, James, *Putting It Together in the Parish* (Nashville: Abingdon Press, 1972), pp. 35–36.

Chapter 4

1. See Donald A. McGavran, *Understanding Church Growth* (Grand Rapids: William B. Eerdmans Publishing Company, 1970), pp. 67 ff.
2. See CGF 9 in the *Manual for Design for Church Growth*, hereafter referred to as the *Manual*.

3. Use CGF 1 in the *Manual* for the collection of this important information.

4. See Ezra Earl Jones, *Strategies for New Churches* (New York: Harper and Row Publishers, 1976), pp. 25–44, for a full discussion of these types.

5. McGavran, *Understanding Church Growth*, p. 85

6. CGF 2 in the *Manual* has been prepared to help you gather the information you need.

7. Peter F. Drucker, *Management* (New York: Harper and Row, Publishers, 1974), p. 45.

8. For a full discussion of the communication problem as it is related to evangelism see James F. Engel and H. Wilbert Norton, *What's Gone Wrong with the Harvest?* (Grand Rapids: Zondervan Publishing House, 1975).

9. See Engel and Norton, *ibid*, pp. 79–102.

10. This is Robert H. Schuller's technique. See *Your Church Has Great Possibilities* (Glendale, Ca.: Regal Books, 1974), pp. 80–82.

11. CGF 2 also provides a form for gathering this information.

12. Chapter 6 describes in detail how to conduct this retreat.

13. W. Dayton Roberts, *Strachan of Costa Rica* (Grand Rapids: William B. Eerdmans Publishing Company, 1971), p. 86.

14. See C. Peter Wagner, *Frontiers in Mission Strategy* (Chicago: Moody Press, 1971), pp. 139–60.

15. C. Peter Wagner, *Your Church Can Grow* (Glendale, Ca.: Regal Books, 1976), pp. 76–77.

16. This is an adaptation from Neil Braun, *Laity Mobilized* (Grand Rapids: William B. Eerdmans Publishing Co., 1971), pp. 128–32.

Chapter 5

1. I am indebted to *Funk and Wagnalls Standard Reference Encyclopedia* which I have followed closely in this paragraph.

2. Donald A. McGavran, *Understanding Church Growth*, p. 84.

3. This data can be collected on CGF 3 of the *Manual*.

4. The AAGR can be computed very easily on a slide rule electronic calculator. The formula to follow is:

$$a = \sqrt[n]{\frac{e}{b}} - 1$$

Code	Calculator Program
a = AAGR	1. enter e ÷ b
n = number of years	2. push $\sqrt[x]{y}$ button
e = ending membership	3. push correct number for n
b = beginning membership	4. push =
	5. − 1 (subtract)
	6. Move decimal two places to the right for AAGR

5. CGF 2, in the *Manual*, when completed will have this data.

6. CGF 5, in the *Manual*, is designed to help you compute AGR.

7. See Ebbie C. Smith, *A Manual for Church Growth Surveys* (South Pasadena, Ca: William Carey Library, 1976), pp. 64–77, for a thorough discussion of the properties and principles of semilogarithmic graph paper and instruction about how you can prepare your own. The *Manual* contains several sheets for your use.

8. CGF 5, in the *Manual*, provide a place for a bar graph to be developed, though a sheet of graph paper may be more convenient.

9. A form for making a leadership profile is included in the *Manual*, CGF 10.

10. CGF 11, in the *Manual* has been prepared to facilitate this analysis.

11. CGF 12, in the *Manual* has been prepared to facilitate this analysis.

Chapter 7

1. George Peters, "Nine Things We Must Do," *Church Growth Bulletin*, Vol. XIII, No. 5, May 1977, p. 127.

2. Ralph Winter, "Who Are the Three Billion?" *Church Growth Bulletin*, Vol. XIII, No. 5, May 1977, p. 123.

3. From lecture given by James L. Sullivan at North Central States' Church Growth Conference, Springfield, Illinois, January 7, 1977.

4. From unpublished material, Evangelism Department, Illinois Baptist State Association, Springfield, Illinois.

5. Richard Sprague, *McCalls Magazine*, March, 1977, p. 158.

6. *Ibid.*

7. Rudiger Reitz, *The Church in Experiment* (Nashville: Abingdon Press, 1969), p. 132.

8. Donald McGavran, *How to Grow a Church* (Glendale, Ca.: G/L Publications, 1973), p. 57.

Chapter 8

1. No one speaks more eloquently or with more authority about the need for and principles for being effective at bridging growth than Oscar I. Romo and his staff in the Language Missions Department of the Home Mission Board, Southern Baptist Convention. See Dr. Romo's paper, "Church Growth Concepts," in "Love Imbues the Mosaic," the reports and lectures of the Catalytic Ethnic Church Growth Conference, held at Glorieta Baptist Conference Center, Glorieta, New Mexico, May 19–22, 1975, pp. 66–68 (Mimeographed). The Language Missions Department staff has produced a number of documents that are required reading for those who wish to do bridging growth effectively: "The Language Mission Manual" (Mimeographed), 135 pages of missions dynamite, "Kaleidoscopic Church Growth Concept" (Mimeographed), and "The World in Our Midst" (Mimeographed).

2. See Charles H. Kraft, "North America's Cultural Challenge," *Christianity Today*, XVII (January 19, 1973), pp. 6–8.

3. Reading a good book on pregnancy and childbirth from the perspective of extension and bridging growth will be a rewarding experience. Try Donna and Roger Ewy, *Preparation for Childbirth* (New York: A Signet Book; New American Library, 1972), Sheldon H. Cherry, *Understanding Pregnancy and Childbirth* (New York: Bantam Books, 1975), or Niles Newton, *The Family Book of Child Care* (New York: Harper and Brothers, Publishers, 1957).

4. The most helpful document in print on this process is Department of Church Extension, *Guide for Establishing New Churches and Missions* (Atlanta: Home Mission Board, SBC, 1972). A slightly revised edition with the subtitle "Evangelizing and Congregationalizing," was issued in 1977.

5. Two documents essential to training the CMC are *The Church Missions Committee Manual* (Atlanta: Home Mission Board, SBC, 1976) and the *Associational Missions Committee Manual* (Atlanta: Home Mission Board, SBC, 1975). No one has produced anything as comprehensive or as high quality as these two manuals. They have both informed the development of this chapter.

6. See John H. Allen, *Associational Missions Committee: Church Extension Planbook* (Atlanta: Home Mission Board, SBC, 1975) for helpful material to guide this kind of group.

7. This is an adaption from Melvin Hodges, *A Guide to Church Planting* (Chicago: Moody Press, 1973), p. 27.

8. See C. B. Hogue, *Love Leaves No Choice* (Waco, Texas: Word Book, 1976), which climaxes with a plea for life-style evangelism.

9. Don F. Mabrey, "The Demand for Dynamic Evangelism," Department of Survey and Special Studies, Home Mission Board, SBC, Atlanta, GA (1973), is essential reading for all persons responsible for or interested in planting a daughter church.

10. Get *Surveying New Communities to Establish New Churches* (Atlanta: Department of Survey and Special Studies, Home Mission Board, SBC, n.d.) for the most comprehensive guide for this process.

11. See Harold E. Cameron, "To Mission Status" (Mimeographed), Missions Department, Illinois Baptist State Association, pp. 2–3.

12. Howard A. Snyder, "The Church as God's Agent in Evangelism," in Douglas, *Let the Earth Hear His Voice*, pp. 332–333.

13. See Harold E. Cameron, "The Chapel Period" (Mimeographed), presented to a Church Extension Colloquium, Southern Baptist Theological Seminary, September, 1974, pp. 2–3.

14. J. Eldon Jones, "The Fellowship Period" (Mimeographed), presented at the Church Extension Colloquium, Southern Baptist Theological Seminary, September 1974, is the most thorough discussion of this stage of new church development that we have read. We have followed him closely in this discussion.

15. See Department of Church Extension, *Mission Fellowships,* (Atlanta: Home Mission Board, SBC, 1976), a tract, for a description of five different models.

16. These are discussed in *Guide for Establishing New Churches and Missions,* pp. 3–7.

Chapter 9

1. See Arn and McGavran, *How to Grow a Church,* pp. 99–124, for their discussion of characteristics of growing churches.

2. See Schuller, *Your Church Has Great Possibilities,* pp. 75–77, for his three tests.

3. John Havlik, with characteristic and obvious simplicity, has identified this threefold process as *making* disciples, *marking* disciples, and *maturing* disciples. *The Evangelistic Church* (Nashville: Convention Press, 1976), p. 15.

4. We are indebted to Lewis Abbott, Pastor of the McArthur Boulevard Baptist Church, Irving, Texas for these insights on Acts 2:41–47.

5. Howard A. Snyder, *The Problem of Wine Skins* (Downers Grove, Illinois: University Press, 1975), p. 139.

6. John R. W. Stott defines the biblical concept "to evangelize" in this restricted manner, but he describes "evangelism" also in wider contexts that include salvation, dialogue, and conversion. See "The Biblical Basis of Evangelism," in Douglas, *Let the Earth Hear His Voice,* pp. 68–71, 76–78.

7. C. Peter Wagner has been the principal advocate of seeing evangelism as a combination of these three elements: proclamation, presence, persuasion. His concept is sometimes called Three-P Evangelism. See *Frontiers in Missionary Strategy,* pp. 124–134.

8. Wagner, *Your Church Can Grow,* pp. 76–81.

9. Schuller, *Your Church Has Great Possibilities,* p. 5.

10. Elvis Marcum, *Outreach: God's Miracle Business* (Nashville: Broadman Press, 1975), pp. 59–60.

Chapter 10

1. Lecture entitled, *Time in Life,* given at a Managing Your Time Seminar, St. Paul, Minnesota, December 1975.

2. Quoted in William H. Cook's, *Success, Motivation, and the Scriptures* (Nashville: Broadman Press, 1974), p. 44.

3. Viktor E. Frankl, *Man's Search for Meaning: An Introduction to Logotheraphy* (Pocket Book Edition; New York: Pocket Books, 1963), p. 104.

4. *Ibid.,* p. 166.

5. Norman Vincent Peale, *The Power of Positive Thinking.* (Greenwich, Conn.: A Fawcett Crest Book; Fawcett Publications, Inc., 1956), p. 97.

6. Norman Vincent Peale, "Keep on Believing in Yourself!" *Success Unlimited,* Vol. 24, No. 5, May, 1977, p. 46.

Appendix

Exhibit A

FUNCTIONAL VALIDITY TEST
FOR CHURCH ORGANIZATIONS

1. WHAT IS THE PURPOSE STATEMENT FOR THE EXISTENCE OF THIS ORGANIZATIONAL UNIT?

2. HAS THIS ORGANIZATIONAL UNIT FUNCTIONED IN ACCORDANCE WITH ITS PURPOSE STATEMENT THIS YEAR?

3. WHAT MEASURABLE GOALS WERE DETERMINED THIS ORGANIZATIONAL UNIT SHOULD ACHIEVE?

4. WERE THOSE MEASURABLE GOALS ACHIEVED? (IF SO, WHY?)   (IF NOT, WHY?)

5. WHAT NONMEASURABLE GOALS WERE DETERMINED THIS ORGANIZATIONAL UNIT SHOULD ACHIEVE?

6. WERE THOSE NONMEASURABLE GOALS ACHIEVED? (IF SO, WHY?)   (IF NOT, WHY?)

7. HOW MUCH FINANCIAL RESOURCE IS REQUIRED TO PROVIDE FOR THE NEEDS OF THIS ORGANIZATIONAL UNIT?

8. HOW DOES THIS ORGANIZATIONAL UNIT CONTRIBUTE TO CHURCH GROWTH?

9. IS THE NATURE OF THIS ORGANIZATIONAL UNIT BASICALLY "MAINTENANCE ORIENTED" OR "OUTREACH ORIENTED"?

10. HOW LONG SHOULD THIS ORGANIZATIONAL UNIT EXIST?

Exhibit B

Productive Prospect Search Form

(Use this form to list your own acquaintances in the various categories)

(Use this form when interviewing acquaintances or contacts)

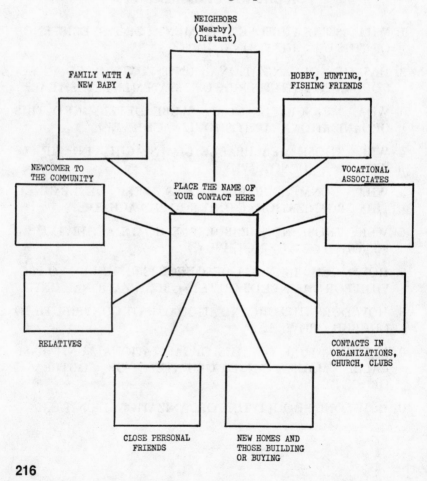

NEIGHBORS
(Nearby)
(Distant)

FAMILY WITH A
NEW BABY

HOBBY, HUNTING,
FISHING FRIENDS

NEWCOMER TO
THE COMMUNITY

VOCATIONAL
ASSOCIATES

PLACE THE NAME OF
YOUR CONTACT HERE

RELATIVES

CONTACTS IN
ORGANIZATIONS,
CHURCH, CLUBS

CLOSE PERSONAL
FRIENDS

NEW HOMES AND
THOSE BUILDING
OR BUYING